The Faith of the
Russian Evangelicals

Books by J. C. Pollock

The Faith of the Russian Evangelicals
Hudson Taylor and Maria
Earth's Remotest End
Moody

51349

The Faith of the Russian Evangelicals

by J. C. Pollock

McGraw-Hill Book Company
New York
Toronto

ACKNOWLEDGMENTS

AMONG those who have greatly helped this book I would especially like to thank Mr. Peter Benenson, Q.C., Secretary of the International Executive of Amnesty International; Mr. S. W. Brooks of Millfield School; Mr. John W. Lawrence, who very kindly came to the Soviet Union at short notice as interpreter; and Dr. Ernest Payne, General Secretary' of the Baptist Union of Great Britain and Ireland.

I am grateful to the Western correspondents in Moscow who gave me advice; and also to the following: Sir Ivor Beauchamp, Bt.; Mr. Robert M. Bowman, President of the Far East Broadcasting Company; Mr. D. C. Cameron; Mrs. Shura Kolarz; Dr. W. O. Lewis and Dr. Clyde W. Taylor of Washington; Pastor Nelson Parr; Alexandra, Lady Studd; and the Librarians and officials of the Great Britain–U.S.S.R. Association, the London Library and Devon County Reference Library.

For kind permission to use copyright material I am indebted to Mr. Maurice Hindus and Victor Gollancz Ltd. and Doubleday and Co. for quotations from *House Without A Roof*, and Mr. Maurice Hindus for a quotation from *Broken Earth*; to Mrs. Elinor Lipper, Messrs. Hollis and Carter and the Henry Regnery Co. for a quotation from *Eleven Years in Soviet Prison Camps*; Mr. John Noble and Glenn D. Everett and Marshall, Morgan and Scott Ltd. and St. Martin's Press for a quotation from *I found God in Soviet Russia*; the Editors of *Current Developments in Eastern European Churches* (Geneva); the Editors of *Current Digest of Soviet Press* (Harvard, Mass.); the Editors and the London Office of *Newsweek*. Copyright quotations from *The Current Digest* are by permission of the publisher. *The Current Digest* is published weekly at Columbia University by the Joint Committee on Slavic Studies appointed by the American Council of Learned Societies and the Social Science Research Council.

J. C. POLLOCK

5

CONTENTS

7

PROLOGUE

LIGHT snow was falling on wide Tchaikovsky Street in Moscow on the morning of January 3rd 1963.

The Russian militiamen (civil police) on duty at the two court-yard entrances of the nine-storey mustard-coloured Embassy of the United States stamped their feet to keep warm despite thick greatcoats, fur caps and *valenkis*, the universal knee-length felt boots. Buses drew up through the slush to the nearby stop, their windows steamed by the heat of packed bodies inside, and drove off towards the underpass and Smolenskaya Place. Down the centre roared a few public corporation trucks, drab and identical, forming most of the mid-winter traffic.

An Embassy car emerged and the militiamen, giving courteous salutes, took lynx-eyed glances at the occupants, ready to give headquarters the customary immediate information on whom had left. As one militiaman stepped into the sentry box to telephone, the other barely noticed sloshing up the sidewalk, with snow sprinkled on nondescript fur caps and skin coats, a group of pedestrians typical of any that had to be out in the freezing Moscow January.

The group, six men, twelve women and fourteen children, some of whom were carried wrapped like cocoons, others hustling at their parents' side, drew opposite the Embassy. Suddenly all thirty-two turned and rushed the entrance. The militiaman struggled, shouted. His comrades ran up from the other gateway and out of the guard box, but by sheer weight of numbers the group pushed through to gain the safety of diplomatic soil. Under the arch formed by part of the building they ran into the doors on either side, some into the administrative offices, others towards the Embassy's community room, still others upstairs, spilling into apartments wherever a door stood open.

Embassy clerks and officials rose astonished from their desks,

9

wives upstairs seized their children at this invasion. And the Thirty Two as they scattered around the Embassy cried out in thick peasant Russian: 'If you believe in Christ and in God—help us!'

.   .   .   .

Next morning the international Press splashed the story and its tragic aftermath by front-page headlines and lengthy accounts— except in Moscow, where *Pravda, Izvestia* and the radio ignored the incident, of which the Soviet public never learned. In London *The Times* made it the lead, printing Reuter's despatch under heading 'RUSSIANS ASK FOR HELP IN FLEEING. Embassy Appeal by Group of 32. Members of Sect Persecuted. 4-day Journey from Siberia.' 'A group,' began the despatch, 'of 32 Russians of an evangelical sect forced their way into the American Embassy compound to-day complaining of religious persecution and pleading to be sent abroad . . .'

In Britain memory of the Siberians was quickly overlaid by the exceptional and Siberian weather which gripped the country in its worst winter for two hundred and thirty-three years. In the United States the story's impact was more lasting. The Embassy was American, the Thirty Two sought refuge on 'American soil'. The tragedy captured the imagination of millions, and when, some six weeks later, an official deputation of Russian religious leaders visited America its members were constantly questioned by the public about the Thirty Two and were unable to answer convincingly, for they were committed to upholding the Soviet Government's interpretation of religious freedom. Moreover, they were themselves mystified; even the evangelical leaders had heard nothing about the incident beyond a deceitful statement from the Soviet Government's Council for Religious Cults.

In the American Embassy in Moscow the memory was raw, leaving almost a sense of having been at a crucifixion.

.   .   .   .

After it was suggested that I investigate the incident I learned that any request to the Soviet authorities to be allowed to talk with the Thirty Two or to visit their home town in Siberia would have met the same response as an attempt to accompany cosmonauts on a trip to the moon. I soon understood also that the incident at the Embassy was not significant in itself so much as symptomatic of a far wider situation which had not begun with the Thirty Two and certainly has continued through 1963 and into 1964. My subsequent travels in the Soviet Union with the courteous aid of the Soviet state agency, Intourist, confirmed that the Thirty Two Siberians were tiny fragments thrown up by an issue which smoulders, sometimes flares, right across the U.S.S.R.

If peace and friendship between Russia and the rest of mankind are to grow true and lasting the world needs to know the grounds and nature of this conflict, which has relevance for very many more than committed Christians. Every man or woman of good will who cares that a fellow human should suffer, whose heart is warmed by the triumph of the human spirit in adversity, should tear aside this particular fold of the Iron Curtain. It is common knowledge that the Soviet Government is atheist; most people are aware vaguely that Christianity still exists in Russia; few appreciate what the issue means to the individual believer.

A writer who is not an expert on Soviet affairs, and does not speak Russian, may seem impertinent in attempting this theme. I do so because of the gap on the shelf. The general reader has nothing. The student may turn to the monumental *Religion in the Soviet Union* (1961) by the late Walter Kolarz, but this extremely detailed work covering all religions was not intended for the general reader. Moreover, for various reasons Walter Kolarz could not give early information about the grave situation which developed in and after 1959; and, a fluent Russian speaker, he was unable for political reasons to visit the country.

For a graphic, easily graspable picture I have limited my scope, in the main but not exclusively, to evangelicals. Partly because the Thirty Two sprang from that background; partly because the average Englishman or American who is not Roman Catholic or Eastern Orthodox would probably be more immediately at home in evangelical services and background than among Russian Orthodox believers; and partly indeed because of the importance of evangelicals for the future. This approach seems right notwithstanding the warm relations between the Russian Orthodox hierarchy and the leaders of the Church of England, and my own happy experiences with Orthodox Christians. On the other hand, the same basic themes that form this book could be worked out in a Russian Orthodox or a Russian Roman Catholic environment or, especially, in one Jewish. The evangelical setting is representative.

To reduce confusion of names I should mention that the major evangelical group is known as the 'All-Union Council of Evangelical Christians/Baptists', being a Union of three denominations, the 'Evangelical Christians', the 'Baptists' and the 'Pentecostalists'. They are often known for short as 'Baptists'. Soviet Press and Government refer to 'Baptists' or 'sectarians', in contradistinction to 'churchmen', which normally applies to Orthodox. The terms 'Baptist' and 'sectarian', however, and that of 'evangelical', have a wider connotation, because many of the evangelical sects and groups did not join the Union.

I found it confusing and still do, for exact and simplified terminology cannot be maintained consistently.

There is one point I must make very clear: of those particular facts and impressions in this book which may reflect adversely on the Soviet Government and its organs, not one was given me by Baptist leaders, pastors, etc., in the U.S.S.R. When they welcomed my wife and me and John Lawrence our interpreter, and gave us warmth of friendship, they did not know I planned a book. We were careful to avoid compromising questions. Should certain circles in Moscow be annoyed at some of my revelations, they need only consult my list of references to find the sources of such information.

PART ONE

CONFRONTATION

CHAPTER I

A KIND OF FREEDOM

KONSTANTIN STEPANOVICH PIRKIN chewed the top of his pen as he sat at the table of the kitchen–living-room of his little home near Rostov-on-Don.

He looked at the blank piece of paper, he looked at the radio, looked at the large unwieldy Bible, the only one he had been able to buy, second-hand from a workmate's family; he looked at his wife ironing and the two children doing homework, and back at the radio again. Should he write the letter he had in mind? Might there follow a difficult interview?

Moscow Radio encourages listeners' letters even on awkward subjects. He poured himself another cup of tea from the samovar and his pen scratched across the paper.

'Atheists often speak about the freedom of conscience which exists in our country, quoting the Constitution of the U.S.S.R., in which it is said that in the U.S.S.R. the Church is separated from the State and the school from the Church to ensure freedom of conscience for citizens. All citizens are free to observe religious rites and to carry on anti-religious propaganda. If,' wrote Pirkin, reaching the core of his problem, 'we are free to observe religious rites, why do we never hear a broadcast from a clergyman?'

Moscow Radio read out his letter aloud on May 24th 1962 and assured him he was 'drawing the wrong conclusion when you allege that freedom of conscience is violated in our country'. The radio speaker, one Y. V. Mayak, declaimed some six turgid paragraphs of prepared script—so it sounded—before Pirkin's question received its answer: 'And finally, Konstantin Stepanovich, why, I ask you, should preachers of religion be given access to a public rostrum? Religion has remained as anti-scientific as it has always been and it is an ideology which is hostile to Marxism. Those who practise religious observances have been and remain our ideological opponents, and to give them access to a rostrum other than in a church or prayer-house would be to further the propaganda of an ideology which is hostile to us. We atheists do not enter a church or prayer-house to give an anti-religious lecture. Why, then, should our radios and television sets, our Houses of Culture, our Red Corners, be turned into temples and our lecturers' desks into pulpits? . . . Religious propaganda—and speeches by preachers cannot be called anything but religious propaganda—are quite unjustifiable violations of the law.'

.   .   .   .

The ordinary Western reader having digested this answer will be puzzled by Moscow Radio's proud claim for 'freedom of conscience' in the U.S.S.R.

The official line goes astoundingly further.

The Soviet Union and other Communist lands, it claims, are the *only areas of the earth's surface to enjoy freedom of conscience in the fullest sense of the term*: 'Freedom of Conscience, like all the other requirements of true democracy, is possible in full measure only in the conditions of a socialist social system.'

Therefore to discover whether in your London suburb or Devonshire village, your New York neighbourhood or Middle Western township, you are truly breathing the pure air of freedom of conscience (in full measure) you need only contrast and compare it with that which you would enjoy in Russia. In Russia there is freedom of worship in church or prayer-house (the term used for evangelical churches) and the priest or minister may preach at the service, provided he scrupulously avoids discussing political matters even if he feels, and his congregation feels, that a serious moral or spiritual issue is involved in some act or intention of the State. But as Moscow Radio pointed out to Konstantin Pirkin, it is an offence against the law for a Christian to propagate his faith outside the walls of church, prayer-house or home. There is, on the other hand, freedom of anti-religious propaganda anywhere and everywhere, inside closed doors or standing on a platform in a park.

Behind this apparent discrimination is the theory that the atheist would be at a disadvantage if both sides could go to the market-place, for the atheist has no church in which to teach and persuade. (The Houses of Culture, Red Corners and clubs do not seem to count; certainly they are little frequented, as the Soviet Press constantly complains.) This, it is held, is freedom in full measure because religious worship is allowed; because the Communist Party's campaign to eradicate religous survivals is officially confined to measures of *persuasion*; and because a citizen is permitted to believe any religion or none at all. Whereas the capitalist world has only a 'sham freedom of conscience', according to no less an authority than the monthly *Sovetskoe Gosudarstvo i Pravo (Soviet State and Law)*. In bourgeois countries 'freedom of conscience reduces itself to freedom of choice of a particular creed, and that only on paper, while in fact it is limited to the privileges of the official creed. That is the nature of bourgeois democracy . . .'

This may be true in Spain. Adherents of any of America's infinite variety of denominations would look up in amazement at such a statement, and so would the American Association for the Advancement of Atheism; and the noisy undergraduate Humanists Society of Oxford University, to say nothing of Bertrand Russell or the Rationalist Press.

Suppose a citizen of Middletown, U.S.A., or Subtopia, England, accepts at face value the assurance that freedom of conscience (in full measure) is to be found only in the Soviet Union and takes his ingrained habits and attitudes with him to live in a small Soviet township. The Orthodox Church building, as it happens, has long been a club with a red flag on the top of its onion-shaped cupola instead of a cross, but an evangelical prayer-house had been opened a few years after the death of Stalin. He joins. After a few weeks he asks why they do not start a Sunday School for the children; he used to teach in one at home. He is informed that to do so would be a criminal offence.

He is aghast, and murmurs '*freedom* of conscience?' The pastor, wishing to prevent misunderstanding, shows him the relevant clauses. They look first at Article 122 of the Criminal Codex[1] in use until 1959: 'The giving of religious instruction to minors or

[1] Of the R.S.F.S.R. (Russian Soviet Federal Socialist Republic). The laws of the other fourteen republics in the Union contained the same clauses.

adolescents in state or private educational establishments and schools or with the violation of the regulations established for this incurs: *corrective labour for a period of up to one year.*' The pastor points out that a Sunday School in a church would count as a 'private educational establishment'.

'But the Codex was in use only until 1959? The clause no longer applies?'

'The clause still applies,' answers the pastor in his precise way, 'because it is covered by Article 142 of the current Criminal Codex, which confirms and maintains five separate clauses of the early Codex. It simply lays down: "The violation of the laws on the separation of the Church from the State and the School from the Church is punished by corrective labour for a period of up to one year or a fine of fifty roubles"—five hundred roubles before the revaluation of 1961. The laws were passed in 1929 and remain in force.'

The next week the Foreigner suggests a Bible Class for teen-agers—he enjoyed the one he had attended as a boy in the West. The answer is 'No', it is an offence against the same article of the Law; and a special Bible study for adults also infringes Article 17 (c) of the Law of 1929.

'Then why not a Youth Group?—sewing for the girls, handi-crafts for the boys, a choral society perhaps, and plenty of games when the snow is off the ground, and you could throw in a religious conclusion; we do this at home and they love it.' He is shown in black and white: 'All such activities by religious asso-ciations and the clergy are illegal . . . Religious associations do not enjoy the right to form circles for artistic self-expression, to arrange concerts, to organize excursions, evenings or assemblies for young people or to undertake other actions which are not con-nected with the celebration of religious rites. Priests and sectarian preachers have no other functions or duties beyond the celebration of religious rites.'

The citizen from Middletown gets thinking. He loves the usual services, the crowded church, the happy singing, but he wants to make matters just like home. 'Why not start a women's group? It is one of the mainstays where I come from.' The pastor, however, is a strictly law-abiding man. Sorrowfully, he turns to the relevant passage which summarizes the position: 'In accordance with the Soviet laws on religion, religious associations may not arrange special prayer and other meetings for women, or form groups, circles, etc., in which women are instructed in religion.'

Towards midsummer when the tall silver birches are in full leaf the Westerner has a brilliant idea. 'Let's have an open-air service, pastor. Everybody come, believers and non-believers. You could invite the atheists to say their stuff and then you could have a go yourself, and the church choir could sing and——' The pastor knows his Criminal Codex. Since all land is State-owned and is the responsibility of some or other State enterprise, the promoters of an open-air religious rally would be indicted under the Article prohibiting 'The conducting of religious ceremonies in State and public institutions and enterprises'. The pastor explains that exception is made for religious service at the request of the dying in hospitals or prisons, and for funerals in cemeteries or crematoriums.

A day or two later the chairman of the local Soviet, a kindly fellow, breathes a word in the Westerner's ear: 'Citizen, it is a little uncultured to go to the prayer-house with that Bible openly visible under your arm. It is wiser to wrap it in newspaper as the others do. A toiler might complain you are trying to persuade people, and I don't want you in trouble. Just a friendly word, Comrade Foreigner.'

Comrade Foreigner is now thoroughly confused by this freedom of conscience (in full measure). He makes one more bright suggestion. 'Why not posters? In New York you sometimes see a huge billboard, with a legend like, "The Family that Prays together, Stays Together." And in California some of the buses have stickers: "Go to Worship this Sunday." They are not so good in Britain. A lugubrious poster of Virgin and Child at Christmas, perhaps; though there is a Bible Text Publicity Mission which buys space in railway stations. And what about a Wayside Pulpit outside the prayer-house itself?'

The pastor, dear man and devoted Christian, true lover of his country and admirer of its social system, does not wish his church to be closed by administrative order. He begs his friend to take such embarrassing suggestions back to the West.

The Foreigner, sadly relinquishing the privileges of life in the one land on earth with freedom of conscience (in full measure), returns to the capitalist world wherein, according to the atheist monthly *Nauka i Religiya (Science and Religion)*, 'freedom of conscience can only exist in such places where it is possible to impose on society such views as are profitable to the bourgeoisie. And what can be more profitable to the bourgeoisie,' asks *Science and Religion* with keen sympathy for citizens of Middletown or Subtopia, 'than religious views, by means of which the bourgeoisie cheats the masses, misleads them, and forces them to reconcile themselves to their unbearable conditions while awaiting a heavenly reward for their patience and meekness?'

·   ·   ·   ·

In December 1962 a Soviet monthly, *Answers to Toilers' Questions*, having repeated the claim that freedom of worship plus freedom of atheistic propaganda totalled the fullest expression of freedom of conscience to be found on earth, uttered a grave admission: 'It must be said that not only people in the West but also many ministers of religion living in our country are not in agreement with such an interpretation of freedom of conscience.'

The magazine argued that the clergy's complaint related to the anti-religious propaganda which 'they consider is incompatible with the concept of complete freedom of conscience and regard as a persecution of religion'; some had even incited their flocks against atheist propagandists. *Answers to Toilers' Questions* missed the point, perhaps deliberately.

An impartial Western observer would suggest that the objection does not lie in atheist propaganda being encouraged and pursued intensely, but in the scales being heavily weighted against Christians, who may neither reply publicly to attacks on their faith and morals nor teach openly, outside their churches and homes, what in all sincerity they believe to be true. If the marketplace were a free forum, if the correspondence columns of *Pravda* and *Izvestia* sometimes carried a Christian viewpoint, as *The Times* carries letters from humanists and reports of atheist affairs when they are hot news; if Moscow Radio would broadcast a genuine debate between Christians and atheists—even were sermons and acts of worship considered too strong a meat—the claim to 'freedom of conscience in full measure' might hold a little more substance.

The very suggestion would make Party and State hold up their hands in horror.

CHAPTER II

'INCOMPATIBLE' . . . 'UNTENABLE'

On March 23rd 1964 a certain Aleksandr Rogov gave a talk on Moscow Home Service on 'The Twentieth Century and the Myths of Religion'.

His would be one of dozens delivered by atheist speakers throughout the Soviet Union. Week by week, month by month such talks pour out over the air. As Pirkin from Rostov had shown, a clergyman can never be heard by home listeners in the Soviet Union. Very occasionally an overseas programme may carry some church dignitary's address, of suitable political or semi-political content, but no Soviet citizen from Kamchatka to Kaliningrad (the former Königsberg in East Prussia), from Murmansk to the Pamirs, will hear a broadcast sermon on a Sunday, or weekday devotional snippets like *Lift up Your Hearts* or the Story, Hymn and Prayer of *Five to Ten*.

Aleksandr Rogov is a professional anti-religious broadcaster, and tape-recordings of his talks are flown for use as far away as Vladivostok Radio. They are very alike; he could compose them in his sleep. Suppose once upon a time, a plane had been delayed and a local broadcaster—call him Ivan—who had never delivered an anti-religious talk before, was told to give one.

Ivan knew that the mass of his listeners would already be atheists, in name at least. As a good Communist he yearned to rescue a few of the uncomfortably large number of Christian believers still existing in 'the world's first state of mass atheism'. He must prepare his talk with utmost care.

An obvious source from which to preach would be the Third Programme of the Communist Party, adopted at the Twenty Second Congress at Moscow in October 1961, the first time Ivan had sat in that wonderful new Palace of Congresses in the Kremlin, air-conditioned, ultra-modern, spacious, comfortable, though to be frank he had enjoyed the Palace more when the curtain rose

22

for the Bolshoi Ballet ... He brought back his reverie from *Swan Lake* to Comrade Khrushchev, stretched across to the bookcase for the Report of the Congress and turned to the Third Programme.

The First Programme, they had been reminded, adopted in 1903 at the Party's Second Congress, in exile, had called on the toilers of Tsarist Russia to overthrow autocracy and establish the Dictatorship of the Proletariat. Achieved in 1917. The Second Programme followed in 1919 at the Eighth Congress and detailed 'the task of building a socialist society in our country. This task was also fulfilled.' The country was now, in fact as in name, a Union of Soviet *Socialist* Republics.

Socialism is not pure Communism. The Third Programme of the Party, 1961, laid down that the next two ten-year periods, the nineteen-sixties and the nineteen-seventies, should achieve the 'mighty and noble end—the building of Communism in our country'. By 1984 the citizens would actually be living under conditions of Communism. Other countries would inevitably follow. The Programme was thus of utmost significance for 'the bright future of the whole human race'.

Ivan had in mind two texts for his anti-religious sermon; two vital themes.

He skimmed through the Third Programme until he reached Section Five: *The Tasks of the Party in the Sphere of Ideology, Education, Instruction, Science and Culture, Sub-section One:* 'In the Field of Development of Communist Consciousness.' He ran his finger down to paragraph (f) *'Elimination of the Survivals of Capitalism in the Minds and Behaviour of the People.* The Party considers it an integral part of its work of Communist education to combat manifestations of bourgeois ideology and morality, and the remnants of private-owner psychology, superstition and prejudices.' As a literary man Ivan rated the language tedious, the meaning sublime. He read on.

'The Party uses ideological media to educate people in the spirit of scientific materialist world conception, to *overcome religious prejudice* without insulting the sentiments of believers.'

Religion must go.

There it was, embedded in the turgid barrage of verbiage

without which the Party could say nothing. Ivan's stubby finger had underlined '*To overcome religious prejudice*'. The Party reaffirmed that it must and would eradicate religion, as a precondition for a pure Communist state. Comrade Khrushchev in his great six-hour speech delivered amid stormy applause at the Congress had specifically stated there could be no compromise. 'Communist education,' he said, 'intends to liberate the human consciousness from all religious prejudices and superstitions which still hamper individuals in the U.S.S.R. from expressing themselves fully.'

Fine words. Their spirit (if Ivan might use such an unmaterialistic word) was summed up and expanded in *Science and Religion*, his favourite monthly, the magazine of the atheists' society, the Society for Knowledge:[1] 'Religion is incompatible with Communism. It is hostile to it . . . The content of the Programme is a death blow to religion, an incontrovertible, completely convincing argument in favour of atheism. It is a programme for the creation of an atheistic society in which people will be rid for ever of the religious bandage round their eyes, of the reliance on the mercy of a non-existent God which fetters a man's will.'

The issue was plain.

.   .   .   .

Unfortunately, thought Ivan, the 'religious bandage' proved thick, remarkably stiff to remove. Further, the Programme reminded Party members that in their struggle to eliminate religion they must use education, not force, they must not 'insult the feelings of believers'. What Stalin had forgotten during the period of the cult of personality, Nikita Sergeyevich Khrushchev had emphasized in his decree of 1954. Do not insult the feelings of believers—expose the machinations, the hypocrisy and greed, the immorality of the conscious propagators of religion, but do not insult the feelings of believers. This made Ivan's task harder, for he had to show that religion was absurd, illogical, unscientific. That took him to his second text. He waded again into the soft mud of the Party's Third Programme: 'It is necessary to conduct

[1] Before June 1963 named the Society for the Propagation of Scientific and Political Knowledge.

regularly broad atheistic propaganda on a scientific basis, to explain patiently'—and again Ivan underlined—'*the untenability of religious beliefs*, which were engendered in the past when people were overawed by the elemental forces and by social oppression, and did not know the real causes of natural and social phenomena'.

Religion was Rubbish.

He had brought his two texts together: 'To overcome religious prejudice' . . . 'The untenability of religious beliefs.' He now needed to fill out his theme convincingly by reference to trustworthy sources if he were to remove the bandage from believers' eyes.

Ivan turned for support to that sure arsenal of effective ammunition, the works of Lenin. Every Soviet citizen revered the memory of the maker of the Revolution, his statue in silver-gilt plaster stood in every town square, in nearly every park. What Lenin said would be listened to with respect.

'Religion is a spiritual gin (or *hooch*) in which the slaves of capital drown their human shape and their claims to any decent life.' Higher up the page Ivan found an even better quote: 'To those who work all their lives, and are in need all their lives, religion teaches humility and patience in their earthly life, consoling them with hope of a heavenly reward. While to those who live off the labour of others, religion teaches charity in their earthly life, giving them a very cheap justification for all their exploiting existence, and selling them tickets to heavenly happiness at suitable prices.' That was good, but Ivan's listeners would not be oppressed and groaning toilers for bloated capitalists; they were free citizens of the glorious Union of Soviet Socialist Republics. Try again: 'Religion is one of the forms of spiritual oppression which lies everywhere on the popular masses crushed by eternal toil for others, by poverty and loneliness.' No good either. Exploited toil, poverty, loneliness were unknown in the Soviet Union, at least in a public broadcast; none of these Leninist quotations fitted the bill.

Ivan reverted to two favourite passages from Lenin which could be eased out of context: '*Every* defence or justification of the idea of God, even the most refined, the best intentioned, is a justification of reaction.' And: 'Every religious idea, every idea of God, even flirting with the idea of God, is unutterable vileness of the most dangerous kind, "contagion" of the most abominable kind. Millions of sins, filthy deeds, acts of violence and *physical* contagions are far less dangerous than the *subtle*, spiritual idea of a God decked out in the smartest ideological costumes.'

Better be a murderer than a believer, better cheat your comrade, rape his wife, than acknowledge God, better syphilis than faith.

Ivan took a tram to the public library.

The *Large Soviet Encyclopaedia*, as each volume appeared over the years, taught the facts as a Party Member should know them. The Encyclopaedia was Ivan's Bible, his Koran, indubitable, indisputable. He turned to the shelves of the Second Edition (the First Edition, pre-war, had been superseded; a glance at the entry under *Stalin* provides sufficient reason) and found Volume 46, published in 1957. He flicked the pages until he reached *Christ*.

'*Christ:* mythical founder of Christianity, supposed to have been born in the Palestinian town of Bethlehem . . . and to have preached in Judaea, Galilee, Samaria and other places a new religious teaching, and who died by crucifixion, and then, according to the Christian teaching, was resurrected.'

Christ was a myth, He never existed, according to the infallible *Large Soviet Encyclopaedia*.

CHAPTER III

WHAT COSMONAUTS FAIL TO SEE

A PROPAGANDIST who sets out to deliver an anti-religious talk which should convince rather than insult soon loses himself in the dreary bog formed by a compound of the Communists' dogmatism on the facts of religion, and their ignorance of what Christianity actually teaches.

The *Large Soviet Encyclopaedia*—having relegated Jesus Christ (and the Sermon on the Mount and the healing of blind Bartimeus and the Last Supper and the Agony in the Garden) to the waxworks, with sticky labels, MYTHICAL, gummed across the nail marks in His hands and feet, the spear wound in His side— applies similar dogmatic treatment[1] to puff away two thousand years of Christian history: '*Christianity*. Christianity, being, like every other religious ideology, a fantastic, distorted reflection of social life, is historically of a transitory nature.' The long article is mainly concerned to show Christianity as an age-old conspiracy against the masses, which now primarily is directed to confronting 'socialism'. The entry on *Missionary Effort* knows all about it: '. . . In the hands of the dominant exploiting classes, missionary effort is a means of enslaving peoples...' Since the Second World War 'the missionary activity of the Vatican and of the outstanding majority of Protestant missionaries is subject chiefly to the interests of American imperialism'.

So the patient attempts to contact the small, murderous tribe of Aucas which ended in 1956 with the deaths of five young Americans on the sandspit of a remote Bolivian river, and the love for her husband's killers which drove Elizabeth Elliott to persevere until she actually lived and taught among them, all was an

---

[1] Cf. *V Pomoshch Politicheskomu Samoobrazovaniya* (*In Aid of Political Self-Education*) for June 1958: '*Most outstanding scholars of the past* have demonstrated . . . that Christ is an invented person who never existed.'! (Italics mine.)

imperialist plot. The New Zealander shot by opium addicts in the mountains of northern Thailand in 1963, mourned by the tribesmen to whom he had brought freedom from fear of demons, was the sinister agent of Wall Street. The countless men and women who leave comfortable homes and successful careers in Europe and America to heal or teach in tropical cities or lonely mountain and jungle outposts have no love for mankind, according to the *Soviet Encyclopaedia*.

This monotonous misconception of motive pervades Soviet writing on religion. The *Atheist's Companion (Sputnik-Ateista)*, one of the most important anti-religious books of 1959, declared that the Ecumenical Movement arose 'for the purpose of undermining the revolutionary movement of the proletariat . . . Through the World Council of Churches the United States exercises pressure on the basic policy of the Protestant Churches in different countries. The World Council of Churches is a religious centre which is interested primarily in political matters. The World Council is hostile to the democratic camp.' *Science and Religion* turned its guns on Dr. Billy Graham in 1961: 'Underneath the cloak of religion Billy Graham is a warmonger conscientiously fulfilling the task set him by his earthly master, Mr. Dollar.'

Far more dangerous than prostitution of motive is atheist confusion about the teachings of the Christian religion.

Aleksandr Rogov once informed his listeners that the Gospel's commandment to love your neighbour had merely superficial resemblance to the great Communist principle that man must be friend, comrade and brother to his fellow man, because 'to a religious person a neighbour is above all a person of the same religion'. All of which suggests Rogov never had read the Parable of the Good Samaritan. Rogov also imagined the Church taught that 'a believer must love his neighbour *in order to save the believer's soul* and win a place for him in paradise', a misreading common among Party members: 'The prime motive for labour now preached among the Baptists', runs an article in *Gudok (Whistle)*,[1] September 5th 1963, 'is self-love, concern for your

[1] The daily newspaper of the Railway Workers' Trade Union and the U.S.S.R. Ministry of Communications.

own "soul" and for its salvation.' The few theological books which filter through the Moscow postal censorship to officially accredited atheist centres are so little understood that the learned magazine *Problems of Philosophy*, published by the Academy of Sciences, in an article in June 1963 with the unconsciously ironical title of 'The Misconceptions of Contemporary Theology', calls Karl Barth the undoubted leader of the Fundamentalists. It is not surprising that the august Academy can perpetrate howlers of simple Christian doctrine: 'According to the Christian view the purpose of life is not to live a good life but to die a holy death, and afterwards to hope for God's mercy. Anyone who doubts His mercy must wait for thousands of years until the archangels blow their trumpets, the dead rise from their graves, and the Day of Judgment dawns.'

Even the works of ex-Professor of Theology A. A. Osipov, the Party's prize exhibit as an ex-Christian, who once taught at the Leningrad Theological Academy of the Orthodox Church and apostasized in 1959, twists and misinterprets. His eagerly awaited book *The Truth About the Catechism* (1963) dabs haphazardly at Christian doctrine. Thus the Lord's Prayer's opening phrase, 'Our Father', evokes the comment, 'A strange sort of father, who threatens his earthly children with the most terrible torture for the slightest misdemeanour', followed by two long pages of close print full of Old Testament curses![1]

Such hash makes little difference. Soviet atheists depend on one great idea: Science has exploded religion.

A clear grasp of Christian teaching is unnecessary, since all religion is a 'collection of fantastic illusions'. Soviet atheists assert that their arguments 'are based on the findings of science'.

'Science' and 'Religion' are irreconcilable, an Either/Or.

.   .   .   .

'Science' is the holy word of the Communists, the spell that

---

[1] When Osipov gave an anti-God lecture in Kiev in December 1963, for which the entrance fee was thirty kopeks, believers in the audience hissed and sent up naughty little notes: 'he has sold himself for thirty pieces of silver' (*Pravda Ukrainy*, December 3rd 1963).

instantly corks the genie of religion in its tarnished bottle, the sun to disperse the murk of the primitive.

Darwin is set on high as the prophet of scientific materialism, his lifelong (if somewhat tenuous) recognition of the Person of God discreetly forgotten, as is his own regret that the Darwinian theories should ever have been used to postulate a mechanical view of the universe. Yet few reputable scientists in the West (as distinct from writers of popular science books) in the second half of the twentieth century would hold that Darwinism as modified by later research and hypothesis had incontestably and infallibly eliminated a Creator. The Communists ignore the long roll of distinguished scientists who were strong Christians, such as Boyle and Kepler and Newton, through Faraday, Kelvin, Pasteur and Ronald Ross, to the present. A Fellow of the Royal Society commented in the nineteen-fifties on the number of Fellows described in the Royal Society Obituary Notices (primarily concerned with their scientific research) 'as having had a deep Christian faith'.

Party propagandists in their zeal to prove that nothing exists which cannot, as it were, be trapped in a test tube, viewed by a telescope or deduced through an electronic computer have prostituted the marvellous technical achievements of the Soviet Union to support atheism. Gagarin's famous remark that since he had not seen God in space no God exists, is scarcely original: back in the nineteen-twenties the aviators who flew at the few thousand feet their planes permitted, well below the cumulus, gave evidence that 'there are no gods because we have been up in the sky and could not find them'. And a cartoon published in 1960, the year before the first spaceman was orbited, show the *Sputnik* and the *Lunik* and a banner: 'We have circled all round the universe and have not found God anywhere.'

As Billy Graham commented on Major Gagarin's statement, it was as if a worm wiggled an inch out of the turf, and since he could not see Comrade Nikita's left boot, concluded no Comrade Nikita exists. Yet the absurdity was trotted out again by the brave and charming Valentina Tereshkova (now Mrs. Nikolayev) during the interview reported in *Izvestia* on July 6th 1963. 'The Holy Scriptures,' she remarked with breathless ignorance, the context being Christianity, not Islam,[1] 'asserts that God's Kingdom is located in the celestial gardens in the heavens. Our cosmonauts have orbited the earth many times, have risen high into the cosmic vastness above the clouds and, believe it or not, have not found any of these celestial gardens.' She said it, *Izvestia*'s correspondent noted, 'laughing gaily'.

Believers laughed too, not gaily, for they felt compassion for Valentina, who had never discovered the Psalmist's experience, 'If I ascend up into Heaven, Thou art there: if I make my bed in hell, behold Thou art there. If I take the wings of the morning and dwell in the uttermost parts of the sea; even there shall Thy hand lead me, and Thy right hand shall hold me.' A very young man called Oleg Obolensky, of the town of Shatura, a Christian and an embryo scientist, courageously sent Moscow Radio an obvious retort to Miss Tereshkova, in a letter which to refute his ideas the announcers read aloud in a schools' broadcast of October 10th 1963.

Oleg's letter, as read by the announcer, began: 'I want to warn you that along with my belief in God, I have faith also in scientific discoveries and the achievements of world science and technology' (at which the programme's expert interjected: 'Previously the Church rejected the achievements of science altogether . . . The Church is now trying to combine its own, that is, religious views, with scientific achievements and discoveries, although this is quite impossible. Well, go on reading . . .') The letter continued: 'If you are surprised that I believe in science and technology, I ask you, has science not proved the heavens are an infinite universe? Everyone knows that cosmonauts and rockets have not penetrated farther than the solar system, and when they do penetrate to other systems only a small distance in the universe will have been covered. You can never embrace the whole universe. You say that Tereshkova flew into the seventh heaven and did not discover any God there.'

At this the expert in the studio, presumably an intelligent man

[1] The interviewer had shown her a book in English about Miss Jerrie Cobb, the American woman pilot training for space flights, and had pointed out a photograph of Miss Cobb at prayer in church. Valentina thought the scene ludicrous (or so *Izvestia* reported).

Gaevskaya made much use of atheistic literature, setting up no less than nine bookshops in the Dnepropetrovsk region and seventy scattered depots. Naturally she had supplies of those modern classics *The Atheists' Handbook* (1959) and *The Bases of Scientific Atheism*, a 455-page textbook published in 1961. She had plenty of more popular material, year by year. In 1962 336 new books and pamphlets of anti-religious content were available through the All-Union Book Chamber in Moscow, reaching a total circulation of nearly 6,000,000 copies.

One of the 336 was specially valuable despite its dreary jacket, on which the title, *The Truth About Sectarianism,* had apparently fallen into the middle of a puddle; for this pamphlet, put out by the Leningrad branch of the atheists' society in a first edition of 23,600, contained the tales of seven who saw the light: N. I. Zyatkov, 'My Break with the Evangelical Christian Baptists'; E. I. Savelyeva, 'Why I left the Dungeon . . .' 'My Lost Youth . . .' etc. An older booklet, published in Moscow in 1960, *'Brothers' and 'Sisters' in Christ,* was a favourite with Gaevskaya because of its cartoons and the attractive picture on the cover: a horrible spider with the face of a grinning, bearded pastor manipulates the strong threads of his web. In one is caught a small boy, in another a fatuous-faced young woman at prayer; two sad men are in the toils and a granny, well meshed, is on her knees. Each chapter describes a sect, whether officially tolerated or banned and illegal. The last chapter is called 'Why We Are Struggling against Sectarianism', and 75,000 copies were put out at the first printing.

Her opponents, Gaevskaya could reflect with satisfaction, were virtually denied this weapon of literature.

Since the limited editions of hymn-books, prayer-books and Bibles published in 1956–57 (two editions of the Bible were issued, one by the Orthodox, one by the Baptists, who were permitted to print 10,000 copies) the Plan[1] had not found possible a further allotment of paper for religious books. The Christians merely had one magazine for each major legal group, its circulation strictly controlled by the Plan, whereas the

[1] The U.S.S.R. has, of course, a planned economy, all production being regulated by a series of Plans.

circulation of anti-religious periodicals totalled over 2,250,000 in 1962.

Dnepropetrovsk's atheist headquarters was a hive of activity and Gaevskaya's fertile mind arranged attractive 'Days' and 'Weeks' of atheism when her teams would descend on factories and collective-farms. She convened, she says, joint meetings of believers and unbelievers, and if she does not seem to have granted believers the right of a public platform, they could ask questions. Her agitators would be waiting afterwards to do 'individual work with believers', earnestly seeking to help them escape the net of religion, to remove the bandage from their eyes.

Out of these hundreds of miscellaneous meetings, these scurryings to and fro and the attendance, dutiful if bored, of the mass of toilers who are nominal atheists together with the 'largest possible number of believers', Gaevskaya could joyfully report success from her wide countryside and teeming city:

(a) Two students in the church seminary have broken with religion and now are mechanics in the Nikolayev Tube factory.

(b) One Baptist, of seventeen years standing, has left the sect in the village of Elizavetinskoe, Petrikovski district.

.   .   .   .

The ratio of effort to result reported from Dnepropetrovsk is paralleled on a nation-wide scale.

Claims are bombastic. *Party Life* (a journal of the Party Central Committee) claimed late in December 1963 that many people had broken with religion and 'hundred and thousands of religious communities have disintegrated'. If this claim be added to similar annual claims in the recent past there must be so little religion left in the Soviet Union that *Party Life*'s next comment is pointless: 'Still greater efforts are needed . . . to make anti-religious work more effective.'

The anti-religious organizations operating in or from Moscow comprise a formidable array. *Izvestia* recently ticked off the list, one by one: 'The Sector of the History of Religion and Atheism of the U.S.S.R. Academy of Sciences' Institute of History; the Anti-religious Sector of the Institute of Philosophy of the same

Academy; the Scientific Atheistic Section attached to the Board of the All Union "Znanie" Society (Society for Knowledge), similar sections attached to the Boards attached to the R.S.F.S.R. "Znanie" Society and the regional, town and district branches of this society; the Scientific Atheistic Section of the Moscow Planetarium; the Scientific Atheistic Editorial Board of the State Publishing House of Political Literature, the journal *Science and Religion*; the Department of Scientific Atheism in the Faculty of Philosophy at Moscow State University; the anti-religious faculty of the city university of Marxism-Leninism and district anti-religious universities, schools, courses and so on.' To top it, a 'House of Atheism' was officially opened on January 30th 1964, in a well-proportioned building off Taganka Square, Moscow, as a club, clearing house and battle school for atheist agitators. Yet *Izvestia* echoes the familiar complaint, 'Our anti-religious propaganda is still far from being as effective as could be desired.'

Inevitably it has occasional effect. *Pravda Ukrainy* quoted a case on January 30th 1964 of a former Baptist called Nikolai S. in the Artificial Fibre Works at Cherkassy who was systematically persuaded for a year by the chairman of his collective and now writes, 'I no longer go to prayer meetings. I curse myself for joining that faith.' The overall picture is different, as snoopers from the Society for Knowledge discovered when they visited three districts of north-west Russia during the summer of 1963. They went first to the Kalinin region between Moscow and Leningrad, where they were told brightly that in 1962 no less than 5,000 atheistic lectures had been delivered. Since each settlement and industrial site in the region should have had at least one lecture, if possible a course of five or six, they asked the number of settlements and sites. The answer was 14,000!

The snoopers moved westward to the Pskov region south of Leningrad. In one village the situation was disgraceful. A Baptist fellowship of eighty-six members met regularly twice a week, but not one atheistic lecture had taken place in 1962, the local club was defunct and the Red Corner had been turned into a firewood store. On their roundabout route back to Moscow they explored the Yaroslavl region on the Upper Volga. In one town, Tutayev, the cupolas of the Orthodox cathedral gleamed with gold paint.

In sight of them stood the House of Culture, a mean and un-attractive building. The woman director was worried about start-ing atheistic evenings. 'When we do hold them,' she said, 'we usually camouflage them under the title of "Songs that help us build and live".'

'As a result,' reported the snoopers, 'the population has a high incidence of religious belief in all three regions. Many inhabitants observe church festivals and carry out religious ceremonies.'

Similar disappointment struck a correspondent of *Pravda Ukrainy*, who described on September 4th 1963 how he had visited a village in the Transcarpathian region. He called at the club and was sorry to learn that only one atheistic lecture had been given in the last six months, about 'The Universe on the Screen'. He went to the house next door and asked the occupier, a collective-farm worker called Shutanich, when he had last been to the club.

'Well, that's a difficult question, because I cannot remember the first time I have ever been there!'

Mr. Shutanich's daughter came in. 'She said, "Oh, no, I'm afraid I could not go to the club. You see, I have a young baby."'

'You don't go to church either, then?'

'Oh, yes, I do. I take the baby with me.'

The baffled correspondent trotted up the street and tried again. The house he called at belonged to a collective-farm tractor-driver, Popovich. Mrs. Popovich explained that she thought the club was for the young, the church for the old.

Her daughter, Mariya, a tenth-former (i.e. aged sixteen to seventeen) at the local school chimed in:

'I didn't go to the last lecture at the club because there was a service at the church that evening.'

The correspondent frowned.

Mariya pouted. 'It isn't forbidden to go to church, is it? In this district even some of the Komsomol members go.'

Since by the Statutes of the Komsomol (the All-Union Leninist Communist Youth League) 'adherence to religious denominations is incompatible' with membership, and every member shall be an active fighter against religious superstitions, this was a scandalous claim, which the correspondent received sceptically.

Enquiry confirmed it. Moreover, a few years back the then secretary of the local Komsomol had happily carried out assignments at the same time for the church council and afterwards became a deacon.

. . . .

F. Baturin was an *anti-religioznik*, a trained professional atheist agitator, who told his sad story in a pamphlet, *I Address Myself to Christians*, in 1962.

He arrived in a rural township, advertised an anti-religious lecture and at the stated time walked into—an empty hall. Next day he announced the lecture again, to be followed by a dance.

The hall was full.

Baturin began his address, and while he mouthed the well-worn phrases which he could have recited in his sleep, proving 'the non-existence of the mythical Christ by the contradictions in the New Testament', he looked about him. Right in front was a flippant girl trying to pretend she paid attention. A young man fidgeted with a hand-rolled cigarette, longing to light up. Most of the audience were schoolchildren wearing the three-pointed bright red neck-scarf of the Pioneers, the girls demure in their curiously Victorian uniform, and Komsomol youths. The few older folk included the bored chairman of the *kolkhoz* (collective-farm), who did not dare miss. Baturin noted to himself, 'The only people who are not here are the religious believers.'

At the end of his lecture he says, 'Any questions?'

An embarrassed silence. Then a voice from the back of the hall calls out, 'It's all clear,' and other voices murmur assent. 'Yes, it's all clear now.'

'But,' says Baturin in a hurt tone, detecting the flippant girl's toes tapping already in anticipation of the dance, 'I know from experience that there are always hecklers who try to get the better of the speaker with their questions!'

A bearded old fellow obliges. 'So the Bible is just a lot of empty talk? Then why does what is written in the Bible come true?'

When asked to exemplify, to Baturin's disappointment the old man merely muttered about birds with iron beaks foreshadowing aeroplanes, and spiders' webs radio, and proved never to have read the Bible and had to be discounted as frivolous.

Baturin used a phrase about 'credulous people'. At which a pert young man in the second row said with an expression of triumph, 'Then why are the churches allowed?' The girl next to him giggled; but a woman in red observed, 'Quite right. In the towns the churches are full to bursting, there are even a lot of young people and Communists there.'

Baturin replied that the churches were kept open for the grannies. 'Are they to deny their faith? . . . As to young people, there are really not so many of them at religious services. Soviet youth is to be found in youth clubs, not in churches. Admittedly there are misguided young men and girls. I appeal to your conscience: young Communists believe neither in God nor the devil, since otherwise they could not be members of the Communist Party . . . Any more questions? . . . Any more questions?'

So disappointing. Baturin had brilliant shots in his locker which he itched to fire at believers, such as, 'If God, as you say, is omnipresent, disembodied, a spirit, why does the Bible assure us that God made man in his own image? For man is not omnipresent, nor is he a spirit!' And: 'Why are there so many contradictions in the Bible? For example, why are the writings on the cross at Golgotha different in each Gospel?' And one shot, specially devastating in Baturin's estimate: 'Is woman a human being or not, according to your Biblical views?'

Instead, the sole result of the lecture was meagre applause, and an indecent haste to clear the benches for the dance. 'Satisfaction?' he asked himself as he left the hall to the dancers. 'None at all. Just another anti-religious lecture, that is all . . . For there was not a single religious believer in the audience.'

Next morning Baturin called at the local Party Office and learned that there were two evangelical prayer-houses in the township. He decided to attend a service and afterwards engage in personal work with individual believers, visiting them one by one.

Walking towards the prayer-house that evening, he reflected with a fervour which echoes that of any Salvation Army lassie or city missionary contemplating the unevangelistic smugness of the average churchgoer, in reverse: 'Hundreds of atheists, a veritable army. If each of them could free a single soul from the toils of religion!'

.　　　.　　　.　　　.

Baturin would have relished the presence of believers in his audience. Most anti-religious agitators dreaded them. In November 1963 *Izvestia* had the story of a respected organization which gave a travel warrant to 'a lecturer who was to speak on the theme of "Science and Religion on the Universe". The cultural organizer at the enterprise where this lecture was planned rang up the lecturer and asked him "take account of the fact that there will be sectarian activists in the audience and so make your speech more specific". And the lecturer . . . returned the warrant with a reference to the fact that he did not consider himself capable of conducting polemics. He could have only said that "Science has proved there is no God".'

Izvestia knew that believers, especially sectarians, who attended atheist propaganda gave the lecturer's arguments, 'a rough reception. And if he, in quoting the Bible or statements by theologians, does not have a correct knowledge of these questions, then the supporters of religion declare in triumph: "What is the point of listening to him? He is criticizing something about which he has no idea."'

More usually believers did not come. 'Atheist propaganda is being carried on without enthusiasm and without perseverance, and is often carried on only among people who are already free from the influence of religion,' stated L. F. Ilichev, Secretary for ideological affairs of the Central Committee of the Communist Party of the Soviet Union at the plenum of the Party in Moscow, on June 18th 1963. He quoted, amid laughter, a priest from Sverdlovsk who said that atheists went to the club for atheist activities, and the church people to the churches and 'neither of us disturb the other', a story which in October was capped by V. V. Grishin, the Trades Union boss in the U.S.S.R.: 'In Taganrog [on the Sea of Azov] in one building is the club of the forging and pressing machinery works and the prayer-house of the sect of the Baptists. They lived harmoniously in the same building. The presbyter of the sect states that the club does not interfere with them, and the atheists "look at films in the club," he says, "and we in our prayer-house read prayers and give praise to the Lord".'

.   .   .   .

Ilichev stated flatly in January 1964: 'Quite a large part of the Soviet people still remain in some degree under the influence of religion.' His words, in an article in *Kommunist*, express the failure of more than forty-five years of atheist propaganda.

The majority of Soviet citizens already call themselves atheists, but Communism will not tolerate indefinitely a believing minority: every individual Christian must be converted to atheism. The comfortable assumption that religion would die out with the older generation has been disproved, and the matter becomes urgent because of the Third Programme's target: all religious belief *must* be eliminated in the course of the next twenty years' preparation for Communism.

The situation is even more critical: 'Wherever we Communists are not active, the influence of churchmen and sectarians grows stronger,' Ilichev has said.

In Western Europe and North America the man who rarely or never goes to church will generally call himself a Christian and may be affronted if told he is not. In the Soviet Union he calls himself an atheist. Both are materialists, indifferent to the prevalent creed, in the West to Faith, in the Soviet Union to No-Faith, and their souls are spiritually a vacuum. In Russia Faith obstinately refused to die: Faith is advancing, as Ilichev admits. To the atheist agitator therefore a Christian is (to adapt the language of evangelism) not only precious for his own sake, to be freed from religious survivals, but for the sake of others he may trap. In Ilichev's words, '. . . the influence of churchmen and sectarians grows stronger'. Which is why he stresses that religion must be opposed: 'We must confront religion with militant, aggressive, scientific-atheist propaganda. The activities of superstitious sects, which are obviously harmful both physically and morally to individuals and to society, must be shown up.'

Educational methods based on a philosophy of atheism have

not succeeded. Soviet newspapers constantly complain of the ineffectiveness, laziness or timidity of propagandists. A detached observer might comment that it is a little like trying to scrub out the stripes on a tiger and complaining of the soap.

The Communist Party is convinced that the stripes can and must be expunged, using clean water—or dirty.

CHAPTER V

MUD

WE were sitting in an airport lounge more than a thousand miles beyond Moscow. The local Baptist pastors and a few elderly laymen retired from employment had come to see us off—simple men, several with long Tolstoyan beards, all with sparkling eyes and some of the kindest faces I have ever seen. They had a grave old-fashioned courtesy about them, a relaxed happiness, tinged with sorrow because this was the hour of farewell.

In another corner of the lounge the girl from Intourist sat with a young American couple who, being of the Jewish faith, had not joined us when we visited the Baptists. The Intourist girl was in her early twenties, a part-time schoolteacher, very charming, well dressed, intelligent and helpful.

She looked across to our group and suddenly exclaimed to the Americans: 'Are those people over there Baptists?'

'Yes.'

'I hate Baptists,' said the girl flatly, and she meant it. 'They kill people!'

'Oh, come, come,' said the Americans.

'Oh yes they do,' retorted the girl vehemently. 'They kill people.'

There could hardly be a more apt comment on the success of a certain sort of anti-religous propaganda.

Back in Moscow a diplomat friend gave me a magazine-type pamphlet of which an edition of 65,000 copies had been issued at the trivial price of forty-two kopeks by the State Political Publishing House, 1962: *'In the World of Nightmare:* a Documentary Photo-Outline of the Pentecostalist-Sectarians.' The photographs give an impression of extremely able photo-reportage. The cameraman seems to have succeeded in taking pictures of sectarian meetings without the participants being aware—and to have peeped right into their homes: children forced to kneel at prayer; a boy

43

locked up alone to learn the Bible; grim old women. A double-page spread shows white robed men and women wading into a river for baptism by hard-faced pastors whose shaven heads have a criminal look. On another page is a wedding; the expression of the bride and bridegroom bears out the caption: 'This young couple is getting married because the sect so decided. Whether they will be happy—this doesn't bother the sect.'

The pamphlet mounts to a climax of horrifying stories: a woman was ordered by a preacher to kill her little daughter 'as a sacrifice to God'; a girl cast herself under a train because her prayers were not answered; a mother tried to throw one child under a speeding truck and to drown the other, as 'human sacrifices to God in the name of "expiation of sins"'; and a grandmother bashed the head of her baby grandchild in with a board, killing it as a sacrifice.

The three last stories concerned one family and were in fact based on a trial held six years earlier, in 1956: the defendants probably not being Pentecostalists at all, but members of a pseudo-Orthodox sect, one of several religious perversions which have lurked beneath the Russian surface for over two hundred years.[1]

The punch of the pamphlet is in its subtle suggestion that atrocities are a natural outcome of sectarian beliefs, that though the 'documentary photo-outline' is of Pentecostalists, all sectarians (i.e. Baptists and all evangelicals) are as bad: 'A sad fate awaits the child born in a sectarian family. He will be denied most of the joys of our happy youngsters.' . . . 'Pleasing the "most high" costs believers dearly' . . . 'By savage rites of witchcraft, without which no religion can exist, the Church enmeshes the believers and gains influence over the imagination, stupefied by biblical tales of "the omniscient" and "the omnipresent".'

The evidence of the pictures looks so conclusive. As page 1 states: 'The facts presented in this outline reveal the ultra-fanatical essence of the sect . . .'

Facts?

One tiny little clue points to a matter otherwise carefully concealed: The authors of the pamphlet are given as 'V. M. Musa-

[1] The problem of these and similar sects will be touched on in later chapters. See Chapter XVIII.

44

tova, a film-director of the Studio of Documentary Films, and cameraman V. P. Troshkin'.

Not one other word hints, let alone discloses, that the photographs are stills from a film of the same name, *In the World of Nightmare*, 'exposing the murderous practices of Adventists' (*sic*). And though the description 'documentary' usually implies photography from real life, all (except for the defendants in the trial of 1956, and for one of an American Pentecostalist) are of actors in the Moscow Film Studio company.

The ordinary Rusisan reader assumes the pictures to be authentic as those of a May Day parade.

.   .   .   .

Alma Ata Film Studio in Kazakhstan produced *The Way Out of Darkness* in 1961 to 'show up the real character of the clergy'. The opening scene shows the Orthodox cathedral at Alma Ata (one of the largest wooden structures in the world) during the Liturgy; within a few minutes two priests are greedily dividing the collection between them so that they can lead an easy life. The scene changes to a nearby street which is being swept, under the eye of a militiaman, by a theological teacher in cassock and pectoral cross, in punishment for misdemeanours unspecified. Thus, states the handout, 'the audience can form their own opinion about the holiness and purity of the Orthodox priests'. The next view is of a famous mosque in Turkestan followed by shots of its mullah selling gems stolen from the structure. As a sideline he runs an 'illegal clinic for sterile women'. Jews are next, shown as in the Alma Ata synagogue. One after another actors strut upon the scene to ape cults and sects, legal and illegal, in discreditable episodes which the film assures its audience are based on facts.

Even if they are, the sins of renegades do not disprove the principles betrayed by them, any more than the crimes of Stalin invalidate (by Party doctrine) the bases of Communism.

The masses bored stiff by straight atheistic teaching absorb stories shown on the screen in *The World of Nightmare, The Way Out of Darkness*, and *Storm Clouds over Borskoye*, which features Pentecostalists. Nearly 30,000,000 people have seen the full-length feature film *The Miraculous Icon* based on the short story which brought fame to the brilliant young writer Vladimir Tendriakov, a tale of a boy who finds an icon of St. Nicholas in a bog and after much suffering caused by his superstitious grandmother is rescued by the schoolteacher, who also gets the best of the argument with the local priest, a character subtly portrayed as a mixture of good intentions, credulity, guile and self-indulgence.

Yet when professional atheists consider the situation the familiar complaint creeps in: 'Many of the interesting films produced during the last few years have not been adequately utilized ... There are not enough anti-religious films of artistic value, because unfortunately literary circles do not show much interest in antireligious efforts.' The Writers Union ignored a letter from *Science and Religion* asking why authors of national standing do not employ atheist themes. In March 1963 only twenty atheist plays were listed in repertoires for the entire U.S.S.R., and in the whole of 1963 only five new atheist films were made. However in *Petrovka 38*, the play about the police in Stalin's time produced early in 1964, the chief bandit is drawn suspiciously like a priest in disguise.

And the prominent composer T. N. Khrennikov, a state prize laureate, has written an anti-Baptist operetta, *A Hundred Devils and One Girl*, about a young reporter on a provincial newspaper whose first assignment is to visit a village where operates a sectarian group. She succeeds in exposing its leader as a swindler. The story was aimed at unmasking the common features of all sects, 'the open money grabbing of the leaders, the aspiration to draw into the sect the greatest number of deceived people, the pharisaical preaching of the observance of God's commandments and the open violation of each of them'. As the chorus kicked and the soprano trilled high notes and the wicked sectarian preached in a thundering bass, a few of the audience at the Moscow Theatre of Operetta might have wondered if this were not insulting the feelings of believers.[1]

· · · ·

[1] To be fair, the Ideological Commission in November 1963 castigated the operetta for this very reason.

Leningrad has its own permanent visual aid—the Anti-God Museum. In the former Kazan Cathedral on the Nevsky Prospect, where Tsar Alexander I spent a night in prayer before the Campaign of 1812, the Academy of Sciences opened a Museum of the History of Religion and Atheism before the Second World War. Now much extended, with a fine collection of beautiful icons and a big library, it attracts a million visitors a year.

The overwhelming impression is of horror. Rack and branding-iron, thumbscrew and whip, authentic relics of the Inquisition, are put to use on lifelike wax-figures, their agonies accentuated by theatrical lighting. Hair shirts and penitential instruments, such as spiked balls to wear next the skin, make the visitor shudder, paintings and caricatures of fat priests and debauched nuns repel, and a Christ distorted by fury drives the Four Horses of the Apocalypse over a carnage of living bodies. (That this Scripture, however unbiblically glossed, should be featured in an anti-God museum has an unconscious irony: in the very next vision St. John saw 'the souls of them that were slain for the word of God and for the testimony that they held; And they cried with a loud voice, saying, How long, O Lord, holy and true . . . ?') The death of Christ Himself is pictured as a ghastly sacrifice to a bloodthirsty tyrant God. And evidence thrust before the visitor leaves no reasonable doubt that across the centuries pain and death have been used by prelate and prince to force men to be baptized, pay tribute, conform.

Many foreigners tour the Museum. One of them aptly summed it up as 'a snake pit of the defamation of religion', depicting not what religion had done to uplift mankind but what man had done to degrade religion. 'A warped, one-sided, insidiously distorted portrait of faith.'

The declared purpose of the Museum 'is to help people who are still under the influence of religion to liberate themselves from it'. A few addle-pated grannies from the countryside might be shocked into abandoning church or burning their icons. Any Orthodox believer of education is aware that organized religion, his own Holy Orthodox Church included, has outlived eras when leaders betrayed the name of Christ and wolves devoured His fold. The Baptist knowing his denomination's history of dissent

47

from the very wickednesses emphasized by the Museum, and remembering that his forebears in Imperial Russia suffered from whips and chains for their faith, is unmoved.

Orthodox and Baptist alike if true believers know (or, to concede a Communist argument, think they know) that the Christ held up to derision and disgust is not the Risen Christ whose Presence is their solace and joy.

Neither of them, being loyal citizens, would harbour the thought that a museum which approached Soviet history in similar fashion could display even more exquisite horror.

.   .   .   .

An anti-God museum affects the comparatively few Soviet citizens who visit it. Newspapers influence almost all, including those who seldom buy them, for a familiar sight in a Russian city, factory or collective-farm is the little group around the board on which the day's papers have been pinned.

The line plugged by newspapers is that Christians are rogues.

A newspaper in the Lithuanian S.S.R., the *Komunismo Shvituris* in the Telshyai region, which opened its pages to churchmen during the summer of 1963 and did not print editorial rebuttal of the statements earned a sharp rebuke, and the local Communist leaders who 'did not notice the flagrant mistake of the newspaper' earned another, from the First Secretary of the Party central committee in the republic, A. J. Snechkus. A paper occasionally prints a letter from a believer (especially if the editor spots a text for an anti-God sermon) or a dignitary's statement, politically correct, or an event of international significance such as the jubilee of the Patriarch. The ordinary run of church news leaves a clear impression on the reader that believers are among the most objectionable creatures in the Soviet Union. Baptists and sectarians are the worst because their laity as well as their clergy are active, whereas the Orthodox laity are less articulate and only the priests usually catch the newspaper's eye.

Christians tend to be immoral or, at the very least, crafty and slippery. Priests and pastors are money grabbers who force their congregations to give and then embezzle the funds, while Baptists hold out a hand for American dollars too (a complete falsehood; nor will they accept them). Christians are mean. Christians collaborated with Germans in the war or fought with nationalist rebels or were conscientious objectors because they cared nothing for their country. They have a horrible habit of getting together in stuffy buildings to sing dreary songs. 'The unctuous sermons and dirty deeds of the sectarians' net the unsuspecting, especially if a citizen is afflicted by bereavement, loss or illness. Once they have laid sooty hands on a man they press and wheedle, bribe and dupe until he is fast caught in their spider-web toils. They are black ravens who spread gloom and despondency. A Christian forces his children to pray and learn Scripture, and when they join the happy games of Soviet schools the parent whips them— which sounds specially nasty to a Russian, who adores children and hardly ever beats his offspring. If a Baptist commits a genuine crime and pastor or church members, who may be his victims, intercede in mitigation, their attempts are described as disgraceful interference with justice. The crime will be written up as natural fruit of his beliefs.

'Self-interest and parasitism, hypocrisy and lack of principle are engendered by the very nature and principle of church life'; therefore to a newspaper any and every action by a Christian has a sinister motive. Christian services are gangster meetings, Christian communities are wasps' nests, adult baptism is a danger to health and Holy Communion, a disgusting custom, an offence to hygiene.

Pravda sometimes admits that newspapers go too far, urges more tact, reminds the provincial Press of Khrushchev's comment that 'being atheists does not give us a right to insult the feelings of believers', and asks for educative propaganda rather than dirt. Journalists find dirt more interesting than atheism and continue to splash Christians with mud or vomit. Without doubt it sticks. The Soviet citizen unless he has Christian friends has a rooted conviction, like that girl at the airport, that Baptists in particular are evil and un-Soviet.

Christians have to breathe a miasma of libel and slander. They accept it as part of their lives. And it is self-defeating, as leading atheists very well know: at a seminar held in 1963 by the Soviet Union of Journalists the Press were warned against publishing 'sensational articles attacking religious people which might create an atmosphere of hostility towards them and *thus strengthen their faith*'.

CONVERSATION PIECE

WHEN agitators gather in the new House of Atheism off Taganka Square in Moscow the conversation may well turn to Baptists, with a fervent wish that neither they nor any evangelical sectarians existed. The Party Programme to eliminate religion by the early nineteen-eighties would be far easier to fulfil.

Comrade L. N. Mitrokhin, a special Party expert, might read to the assembled company his article of February 1964, *Some Features of Modern Baptistism*, or quote from another of 1960 in which he establishes that Evangelical Christians/Baptists are more numerous than all other non-Orthodox combined, with a large number of preachers who have 'latterly become noticeably more active'. Mitrokhin admits 'an increase in the number of Baptist communities in some areas . . . Not only the heads of the communities but also many of the ordinary sectarians try to spread their religious beliefs.' The ideological fight against the Baptist creed is urgent. Because, says Mitrokhin, it is a 'religion which is pruned, refined, more subtle'.

Another expert, E. F. Muravyev, expounds again his conviction that believers in Russia fall into two classes, 'formalists' and 'fanatics'. The 'formalists' include much of the laity of the Russian Orthodox Church: they observe rites and ceremonies 'as a matter of tradition rather than conviction' (though many participate more deeply than Muravyev is aware). 'They call themselves believers but do not impose their beliefs on other people and are tolerant towards atheism.' On the other hand, 'the fanatical believer actively propagates and defends his views, sincerely convinced of the truth of religious teaching and trying to observe its principles in his daily life. These people,' states Muravyev, 'are mainly sectarians for whom religion is a deep inner conviction.'

A third agitator, in from Siberia and unknown by name to the others, frankly tells them what he said to a Russian-speaking

American journalist visiting Irkutsk: 'You don't have to argue with Baptists as with Orthodox about icons, relics, incense swinging. They repudiate these as firmly as we Communists do. Nor is there anything you can tell them about the evils of drunkenness, hooliganism, wife-beating—oh, they're strongly against it and teach it to their children. When you throw scientific facts at them, they do not dispute you. They're all for science, they tell you, and for all the good it does for mankind. But they always tell you that the laws of science are God's laws, and when you ask them whether they have ever seen God or spoken to Him, they tell you that God is within them, they feel it and rejoice in it, it inspires them to be good and do good and to live not only for themselves but for others.'

'They're so stubborn,' concludes the agitator from Irkutsk, 'about feeling God inside themselves that you cannot root it out of them.'

The company agrees. The agitators turn from unpalatable truths to rub up their slogans.

'The Baptists consistently poison the minds of children and trample on their wills,' says K. Oya, from Estonia, quoting an article he had written in August 1963.

'A good Baptist should only believe, he should not think,' someone quotes from *Criticism of Religious Ideology*, published in 1962.

Another quotes from *In the World of Nightmare*. 'What won't people do for money!'

.   .   .   .

Without doubt the Baptists and other evangelicals cannot, at the very least, be ignored; in less guarded moments atheists even admit that 'fanatical' believers are seizing the initiative. In the confrontation of massively State-aided atheism with the religion of humble individuals seeking nothing but to worship and serve God according to their conscience, the Baptist-Evangelicals play a significant part.

It is time therefore to look at the confrontation from their side, to explore their ways and cast of thought, their reactions, problems, tensions; to see how they exert their influence at almost all levels of Soviet life; before turning to the immediate causes of the agonized eruption of the Thirty Two Siberians into the American Embassy.

For all this to make much sense a delve into the past is necessary, to discover how a strong evangelical Church arose in a land predominantly Orthodox. The several Communist treatises on the subject are of interest to Baptist historians only, who might enjoy them as parodies; the true story has significance for all lovers of freedom whatever their religion.

Briefly, then, the page must be turned back a hundred years and more, back to over a decade before Lenin was born. The Communist Manifesto was a bare ten years old and forgotten, Karl Marx, scarcely known, sat grubbing at obscure books in the British Museum; the United States was absorbed in the mounting crisis leading to the Civil War, the British Empire busy with the aftermath of the Indian Mutiny; and the fields of the Crimea were still littered with relics of the recent war.

PART TWO

FLAME ON THE STEPPES

CHAPTER VI

MICHAEL THE SERF

MICHAEL RATUSHNY was a serf. Like the others in the village of Osnova in southern Russia not far from Odessa, he expected to live out his years tilling the soil, tied to the land where he was born.

With blue eyes, mouse-coloured hair and bushy, silky beard which had never known a razor, he was tall and at twenty-three or four had not yet filled out to the typical girth of his race. He was as illiterate as his neighbours and the millions of their kind throughout the Tsarist Empire, his hut was dirty, his days as dreary as the landscape.

The *muzhiks* or peasants of Osnova in the later eighteen-fifties had an advantage over many: their landlord let them hire themselves at harvest to farmers of the German colony nearby, one of those planted in the Ukraine by Catherine the Great in the eighteenth century which kept their German identity, customs and rights until broken in the Soviet collectivization and forcibly deported and scattered during and after the Second World War. The Germans were kind employers, their houses bright and clean, their farms efficient.

The colonists had brought with them a strong evangelical faith. They were free to worship as they wished; on no account might they proselytize among the Russians, sons of the Orthodox Church, which demanded, and outwardly received from all but a fraction, the allegiance of every Slav. But the Russian Orthodox Church had fossilized. The depth of spirituality inherent in its Eastern Christianity had been smothered. Visitors to the Soviet Union today who have shared the devotion and joy of a Church purged by the fires of the twentieth century will find its picture in the mid-nineteenth astonishing. In most country churches with their onion-shaped cupolas topped by crosses the Liturgy had become a meaningless jumble of an archaic tongue, the icons in church and home instead of being pictures and carvings to focus the mind on the Deity were themselves worshipped; the 103 annual church festivals became drinking sprees; popular belief was a maze of pagan superstition in Christian dress, and the priests, the village 'popes', were all too often ignorant semi-illiterates following a family calling and battening on the ecclesiastical dues of their flocks.

To Michael Ratushny, each harvest, the simple piety of his German employers seemed some bright song from a distant heaven. He could not understand German, but he and his friend Onishenko would stand far away on the warm summer evenings when the farmers gathered for their *stunden* or Bible hours and would listen to the hymns and the peaceful murmur of old Pastor Bohnkemper's reading and expounding.

One harvest time Bohnkemper dared to break the law by inviting the Russians to join the *stunden*. He sent to St. Petersburg for New Testaments and began laboriously to teach the two serfs to read Russian; there was no Bible in their native Ukrainian. Each evening the lessons continued; each *stund* the serfs worshipped; when they returned to Osnova for the winter Ivan Onishenko had a new outlook on life. Ratushny groped confused and yearning.

On a winter evening the *mir* or village meeting gathered round the stove in the largest hut, the air thick with tobacco smoke and the stench of greasy blouses. Matters of business were disposed of and the usual interminable discussion about anything or nothing began. A villager asked the priest the meaning of these strange teachings that Ivan and Michael had heard in the *stunden*. 'What does it mean, little father, when the Gospels say, "You must be born again"?'

'Yes,' said another villager. 'Ivan Sergeivitch talks of the blessed Apostle Paul writing, "By grace you are saved through faith. It is the gift of God." Ivan cannot tell us what this means, but he is a happy man now. What does it mean, little father?'

The priest mumbled. He grew rather cross. He had never bothered to think.

Then Michael Ratushny 'felt within himself a burning desire to understand God's words with my own mind, and to explain them to others'. He began to speak. Confused at first, he talked of what he had heard, and the truth suddenly clicked, his mind cleared, his heart warmed just as that of John Wesley, so utterly different in background and education, had warmed in London's Aldersgate Street the century before. This was his Damascus Road; this was conversion. It was also a climacteric of history, for Onishenko seems to have been a bovine man (most of the accounts ignore him) of unapostolic mould.

Not that Ratushny set out to be an apostle. The priest sent for the police because Michael now refused to worship the icons. 'When I was cast into prison,' Michael relates, 'all knew that I was locked up because I had read the Gospels. They wondered exceedingly, and all who could read procured the Gospels and began to read for themselves.'

Alexander II, the new Tsar, had revoked his father's ban on the distribution of Bibles; this and the brief life of the earlier Russian Bible Society founded by Alexander I in 1812 but suppressed by Nicholas I as subversive had prepared the soil for the 'Stundists', as Ratushny and his converts were soon known. Russia alone of Eastern Orthodox countries had become a Bible-reading, or at least Bible-venerating nation. Especially among the Old Believers, descendants of those who had refused to accept certain liturgical reforms and modernizations in the seventeenth century, thus creating the Great Schism and retreating into a rigid conservatism, many studied the Bible, such as the Old Believer priest who, coming across the works of Luther, discovered that he himself had made independent discovery of Justification by Faith.

The priest later became a Stundist. Like all religious movements, Stundism had been long preparing unawares. Ratushny's conversion was the spark that lit the fire.

.   .   .   .

In 1861 Alexander II set the serfs free. The Emancipation was a vital factor in the rise of Stundism, for after it *muzhiks* could travel more easily.

Ratushny (whose brief first imprisonment of a few days did not cool his heels), Onishenko and others would tramp from village to village after harvest, disguised as pedlars or book hawkers, travelling, as any *muzhik* did, with no gear but a wooden spoon tucked in one leg, a comb in the other. A scout would go ahead and warn outlying hamlets. The peasants gathered at a remote cottage or a hidden hollow, and would listen for hours. 'Icons are dead and useless!' the Stundists proclaimed. 'It is wicked to worship them; the Holy Bible says so. God alone must be worshipped, and He is in heaven. Jesus is the Saviour of us all, and not St. Nicholas or St. Andrew or St. Jonah. He who truly repents need not confess his sins to the "pope". Jesus will forgive our sins without our paying for Masses. Lying and drunkenness and theft and swearing, these are sins, brothers and sisters, to be repented of and put away. No true Christian lives in such sins, which God hates.'

The message fell on hungry minds to meet a deep urge which Orthodoxy had failed to satisfy. One man had yearned and panted as he stood in the crowded village church while the Eucharist was sung beyond the royal doors. Afterwards he begged the priest, 'Speak to me, father, and explain to me, for kindness' sake, everything according to the Scriptures.' The priest replied with abuse. 'Go away from me, you heretic!' Another man heard a small boy read from the New Testament 'and I felt that I must forsake evil behaviour and live a righteous life'.

It was all spontaneous, fervent and rather chaotic. Pastor Bohnkemper's son returned from America, where he had emigrated to seek a fortune but had become a minister, and stepped into his father's shoes. His guidance was often sought, yet the leadership lay with the peasants. Each group was independent, linked by brotherly love, divided by differences on a score of minor matters, united by hunger to live according to the New Testament and by the overwhelming knowledge that God's Spirit is no preserve of priests but may dwell in the poorest, most ignorant *muzhik*.

The Stundists proved it by their lives. Gentry visiting a Stundist's hut were astonished. They saw a cleanliness unheard of in Russian villages. They found kindness to animals, even to pigs. The Stundist had renounced alcohol, that curse of the peasantry. His wife no longer a buffeted slattern, but the honoured mistress of a household, her head-scarf and blouse clean, her face scrubbed and bright as her eyes. Every Stundist had a passion for education, for the ability to read was the gate to the world of the New Testament; those who were too old or dull to read would memorize whole chapters. In the long winter nights any who had learned taught others, spelling out the words verse by verse, and in summer young men took their Testaments to the fields to read during the meal break, or to prove the truth to fellow labourers. Every convert became a missionary.

And they sang. From the first Stundism expressed itself in song. They used the old Russian hymns, changing the words where necessary; they took German chorales learned from the colonists and sang them in the slow mode of Orthodox congregational chants, they paraphrased Scripture verses and set them to folk songs or made up their own tunes, joyful or stirring or sad, with complicated parts and tempo changes such as only Russians can sing with accuracy and verve. In due time they even had translations of Moody and Sankey. Native or borrowed, chanted or free-style, Stundist singing released Stundist joy.

.　　　.　　　.　　　.

On an evening of 1867 in the village of Lubomirka a blacksmith called Ivan Rjaboshapka, who had already roamed the steppes telling how 'I once walked in darkness but I have seen the light', gathered half a dozen neighbours in his hut. He read aloud slowly from the Epistle to the Ephesians: 'Put all bitterness, and wrath, and anger, and clamour and evil speaking away from you, all malice too: and be kind one to another, tenderhearted, forgiving one another, even as God for Christ's sake has forgiven you.'

The candle spluttered. The door kicked open. Three policemen strode into the room while the village priest waited outside. Ivan Rjaboshapka stood up uncertainly. The senior policeman sharply announced that everyone in the room was under arrest for holding an illegal meeting.

Orthodox Church and Tsarist State were warp and woof of Holy Russia, with State firmly master of Church. The imperial government regarded unauthorized dissent as virtual disloyalty. The reigning Autocrat of All the Russias by his liberal policy had unwittingly allowed Stundism to flourish, but Ivan Rjaboshapka and his friends were about to receive a taste, as others already had, of the Stundists' fate should reaction return and local priestly hatred and the whim of an antagonistic Governor be authenticated by clear orders from the Tsar.

61

The policeman looked around and seized an old woman of seventy. He had her bared to the waist and tied face down on a bench. His assistants gave her eighteen strokes with rods. Ivan's other listeners, harrowed by her screams, were birched themselves, then Ivan was ordered to strip naked. The village blacksmith was a muscular man in the prime of manhood, but the policemen flogged him until he was half-conscious and blood dripped on the ground, the priest gleefully urging them on: 'Beat him to death! He deserves it. He is a son of Satan!'

After the police had gone Ivan murmured: 'It burned, yes it burned. But it was nothing to the fire of Jesus' love in my heart.'

.   .   .   .

The persecution soon to break out might have burned Stundism to cinders had not a similar movement arisen farther south-east in the Caucasus.

It arose from a complicated background. For many generations there had been religious dissent in Russia. The miscellany collectively known as Old Believers had entrenched themselves in a dissenting Orthodoxy even more petrified than that of the State Church; behind and beyond practised in secret a variety of peculiar sects, born of protest and nurtured on the surmises of mad or roguish prophets. Some had innocent if fantastic beliefs and rites; two, the Flagellants and the Sect of the Castrated, whose adherents were drawn from all classes, undoubtedly perpetrated abominations: ritual castrations of youths, babies sacrificed for ghastly Eucharists of human blood. Such pseudo-Christian aberrations have survived in backwaters to bedevil the later twentieth century.

The *Dukhobors* ('Spirit-Wrestlers'), known in the West because in the last years of Tsardom many emigrated to Canada, where they have tried the patience of the authorities, used Christian terms unanchored to Christian meaning. From the Dukhobors, however, sprang the far larger sect of the 'Spiritual Christians' nicknamed *Molokans* or 'Milk People' because, it is said, they drank milk on days when the Orthodox Church forbade it. The Molokans sought to make the whole Bible their sole rule of conduct and belief, yet had evolved an outlook loosely akin to that of a Unitarian Quaker with Mosaic overtones. The Molokans (and the Dukhobors) had been deported to the remote undeveloped Transcaucasus in 1841, and soon were living in prosperous villages of their own and in neighbouring towns, allowed a measure of religious freedom and local government.

Among them in the eighteen-sixties in the beautiful city of Tiflis, where Stalin was to be born a few years later, lived a Molokan leader called Voronin.

Nikita Voronin was a merchant of substance. After he had closed his account books in his cool, pleasantly furnished home each evening he opened the large fat Bible which every Molokan possessed but few read. Voronin developed a passion for understanding: the book became alive under his eyes, and he found much that was disquieting. The Molokans in their hazy way assumed that a Molokan by birth or adherence had a valid passport to heaven: the Bible spoke differently. Molokans welcomed new disciples but would not stir to win them: the Bible, as Voronin turned the pages of the New Testament, appeared to demand that a Christian should be an evangelist whatever the cost. The Molokans eschewed all sacraments: the Bible showed that all who believed were baptized.

He read himself into an understanding and an experience which made him feel close kinship to St. Paul and out of harmony with Molokans.

The merchant Voronin would have instantly recognized the *muzhik* Ratushny as his brother, but the two were 700 miles apart unaware of each other's existence.

In Tiflis lived a German craftsman, Martin Kalweit, an emigrant from the Russian province of Lithuania, who with a handful of his relations and German friends squeezed a little Baptist church into his parlour. Voronin met him and on August 20th 1867 in the River Kura the craftsman baptized the merchant.

For four years the 'Russian Baptist Church' founded by Kalweit and Voronin remained little more than a name until in 1871 Voronin baptized two young men of Molokan stock, Vasily Pavlov, a slim seventeen, and V. V. Ivanov-Klishnikov, who at twenty-five quickly determined that smug Molokans should become New Testament Christians. The zeal and abandon of

who was used to hearing little except flattery from his peers and fawning from his inferiors, dawned an uncomfortable conviction that life hitherto had been selfish, worthless and vain.

As the unimposing stranger talked on, Christ's death and resurrection leaped into relevance. The Holy Spirit became an intensely personal reality. Though the speaker did not attack the Orthodox Church, his simple words contrasted sharply with the ornate ritual of richly vested priests in St. Isaac's Cathedral. Colonel Paschkoff leaned across to his neighbour, a prince, and whispered urgently, 'Who is this man? I must talk with him. Who is he?'

'Lord Radstock. An English milord. The Grand Duchess met him in Paris. She's been a different woman since.'

That night, kneeling beside Lord Radstock with a Bible open between them, Colonel Paschkoff became spiritual brother to Ratushny the *muzhik* and Voronin the merchant.

Others followed, such as Count Korff, the Tsar's *Maître de la Cour*. Count Brobrinsky, the clever and cynical Minister of the Interior, had no such leanings. His wife had got herself mixed up in what he considered the ridiculous 'drawing-room revival', and he was annoyed when she invited the cause of the trouble to dinner. Brobrinsky had enjoyed the latest novel, a brilliant skit called *Lord Apostol*, yet had no wish to meet the tiresome man it caricatured. To stay away would have been insulting, and he listened with half-amused tolerance while Lord Radstock, with blithe disregard of fashionable taboos, turned the conversation at table to religion. The caviare, the little pies, slivers of sturgeon and all the other delights of *zakuski* came and went, the great roast arrived, was served and still the company, except the host, sat enthralled by a disquisition on the Epistle to the Romans. After the ice puddings Brobrinsky excused himself on pressure of public business, retired to his study and wrote a refutation of Radstock. The brilliant essay went to the printers.

In the next few days Brobrinsky was haunted by the calm certainty he had detected in Radstock's eyes and speech. The printer's proofs arrived, the agnostic Minister of the Interior shut himself in his study and began to look over what he had reckoned an unassailable argument to demonstrate that the Deity, if existing, was unknowable. As Brobrinsky read, something snapped:

66

'Like a sudden flash of light in my soul I found that Jesus was the key, the Beginning and the End.'

Brobrinsky's palace and his country estates, like those of Korff and Paschkoff, became centres of the new evangelical movement and models of agricultural and humane reform.

. . . . .

Granville Waldegrave, third Lord Radstock, was just forty when he came to St. Petersburg. His grandfather had been one of Nelson's admirals. The young Lord Radstock had been swept into the fresh wave of evangelical revival which had crossed from America to Britain in the late eighteen-fifties, and he and his wife, a noted beauty, would hold Bible readings for the aristocracy in the drawing-room of their London house. He founded mission halls and refuge centres in the slums and moved unobtrusively, devoted to his purpose, among rich and poor. His best work was done out of England. Taking opportunities as they came, this unusual nobleman grew to be an influence among his class in Holland, then in Paris and thus, through a visiting Grand Duchess who invited him to St. Petersburg, in Russia, where his name passed into history.

Dostoievsky heard Radstock preach in 1873. 'I found nothing startling,' he wrote in his *Diary of a Writer* (1876). 'He spoke neither particularly cleverly or in a particularly dull manner. But yet he performs miracles over human hearts; people are flocking around him, many of them are astounded; they are looking for the poor, in order as quickly as possible to bestow benefits upon them; they are almost ready to give away their fortunes . . . He does produce extraordinary transformations and inspires in the hearts of his followers magnanimous sentiments.' The Radstock revival had incalculable possibilities for Russia. Many of the educated classes were intensely religious yet unsatisfied by the detached formalism which encrusted the Orthodox Church; they were intensely patriotic yet disturbed by Russia's monolithic, repressive political system and by 'the segregation', as Dostoievsky called it, 'of the educated strata of society, our detachment from our own soil, from the nation'. The evangelical revival could have done much to end this fatal detachment, for nobles and *muzhiks*

67

met as brothers. Here was a better road than that of Nihilist revolutionaries.

The wrath of the Orthodox Church was aroused.

The pattern was repeated. What might have been a reformation within the Church was forced to be a sect outside it; the informal groups of all classes which gathered round Paschkoff, Brobrinsky and other friends of Lord Radstock in St. Petersburg and in their country estates became known as 'Evangelical Christians'. Leadership lay with nobles and gentry, and at first they were protected by their position. 'Leave my widows alone!' the Tsar replied when Church authorities wished to proceed against Princess Lieven, in whose palace the St. Petersburg Evangelical Christians held their services.

In 1881 Alexander II was blown to pieces by a Nihilist bomb. He had been on the verge of granting a further measure of political freedom and religious toleration. His son Alexander III answered his father's murder by stark reaction.

CHAPTER VIII

HIGHWAY OF SORROW

IN 1884 Colonel Paschkoff convened a united evangelical conference. He had travelled widely in Russia, knew many Stundists and Baptists, and some 400 delegates converged on St. Petersburg. Paschkoff hired a hotel and gave them hospitality, having already paid their fares. They met in a hall in Princess Lieven's palace where every servant was a convert except the surly old *dvornik* or doorkeeper.

Representatives of the three major strands of Russian evangelicalism, the Stundists, the Baptists and the Evangelical Christians, joined in prayer and praise. Each strand was of different origin, but a classic example of the spontaneous expansion of the Church: Christians from another nation had touched off a movement which propagated itself, thoroughly indigenous in leadership and character. The three movements, unrelated yet emerging almost simultaneously, affected North and South, the illiterate peasants, the merchants, the nobility. It is not fantastic to imagine that this evangelical revival, widespread, gathering momentum, might have deflected the course of Russian history.

The conference of 1884 continued happily for three or four days. On the next no provincial delegate appeared. Princess Lieven, Colonel Paschkoff and their aristocratic allies were puzzled by the disappearance of these men far from their homes. The hotel was empty. Two days later a scared *muzhik* delegate slipped into the palace. He told how they had been arrested shortly after leaving the conference. In the fortress of St. Peter and St. Paul they had been searched and questioned. Some of them were told that revolutionary literature had been seized from the others, at which they laughed. 'The only revolutionary document possessed or used by any of us is the Bible! We aim at no revolution other than that which the cross of our Lord Jesus Christ effects.'

Police had escorted them to railway stations for despatch home at government expense; the *muzhik* who gave the news to Paschkoff had cannily asked for a ticket to a place near St. Petersburg and had doubled back at risk of arrest and punishment.

The collapse of the conference was a prelude to an intense and violent persecution in which Church and State vied to suppress the evangelicals. Princess Lieven had to retire to her estates. Paschkoff was banished. When, on petition to the Tsar, he was allowed a brief return to settle his affairs Alexander III soon peremptorily ordered him to private audience.

'I hear you have resumed your old practices!'

'My friends have certainly called to greet me, and we have prayed and read the Word of God together . . .'

'Which you know perfectly well I will not permit. I will not have you defy me. If I had thought you would repeat your offences I should not have allowed you to return. Get out. And never set foot in Russia again.'

No such mild fate awaited the majority of the evangelical leaders. They were harried, persecuted, imprisoned, exiled to Siberia, Transcaucasia or other barren confines of the Empire. Not being men of rank, they were treated as any criminals—beards and hair half-shaved, wrists and ankles shackled by heavy chains—they were driven across mountains and deserts beside bandits, swindlers and rapists. They suffered worse than Lenin and most revolutionaries whose exile was unmarred by flogging, hard labour or the treadmill. Their wives would have been destitute without the charity of their fellow-Stundists; when a man's sentence was served he would be kept in exile by administrative order and his family could sometimes join him—travelling under such inhumane conditions that women and children often died on the road. It was indeed *The Highway of Sorrow in the Nineteenth Century*, the apt title of an Englishwoman's novel based on reliable evidence.

Faith was bent and tested. That of a few broke. That of most proved gloriously resilient. 'How good the Lord is,' exclaimed Paschkoff's Inspector of Forests at the start of the march to Siberia, 'I have been praying to work among the prisoners and this is how my prayer is answered.' 'We have heard from some of these martyrs since their arrival in Siberia,' wrote the London *Christian World* in 1893 of seven Stundists from Kherson province, 'and they are full of a magnificent hope that even in their distant homes they will be shown a way to spread the light of the coming Kingdom.' The effect was similar to the first days of the Church, when Saul made havoc and 'they that were scattered abroad went everywhere preaching the Word'. The persecuted Russian Christians bred churches wherever they went.

In the Ukraine and other Stundist areas groups continued to meet in secret. Some of the ignorant, deprived of their leaders, developed strange ideas and slithered into the shadow-world of peculiar sects, but the desire to live according to the teaching of the New Testament, and the Old as understood by the New, kept simple peasants and workmen in harmony with historic Christianity. As in the days of the catacombs, the more faith was persecuted, the firmer it grew. One village Bible reading was surprised by the police. Among those attending was a young man who had been feeling his way to belief; he had not yet fully joined the group. At the police station he was strapped to the flogging bench and beaten hard. 'This is for seeking my Saviour lazily,' he had the temerity to tell the police as he put on his clothes again. 'I will now seek Him with my whole heart and cling in spirit to His pierced feet on Golgotha, and hold Him fast till death.'

.   .   .   .

If exiles and prisoners won converts among their fellow-sufferers the evangelical movement was greatly aided by the zeal with which the Tsarist government, with Russian illogicality, encouraged the distribution of the Scriptures in prisons, accompanied by preaching as strong as that of any Stundist, by the representatives of the British and Foreign Bible Society.

The man whose name must be for ever associated with this enterprise (although not an official of the Bible Society) was William Frederick Baedeker, a German-born naturalized Englishman, cousin to the maker of the famous Baedeker guides, and a convert of Lord Radstock. Dr. Baedeker travelled throughout Russia and twice traversed Siberia, met prisoners on the march, stayed in exile settlements. Carrying a mandate from St. Petersburg stating he lay 'under special command to visit the Siberian prisons and to supply the convicts with copies of the Holy Scriptures', he was given every official aid, and often a prison governor would stand beside him as he distributed Bibles or preached. 'Dr. Baedeker was always received,' noted an Englishman who once accompanied him, 'not only with the respect due to the authority by which he came, but with courtesy and appreciation of the object of his coming.'

He could converse in Russian, but preached through interpreters using English, German or French. Tolstoy wrote of him that 'he speaks in such a way that the most hardened criminals sink on their knees, and weep, and repent'. Baedeker brought encouragement to persecuted Stundists, hope and comfort to innumerable convicts, whether felons or politicals, though few revolutionaries responded to his message. In Siberia many of the evangelical churches of the nineteen-sixties have their distant, often forgotten origin in the apostolic labours of the gentle and indefatigable Dr. Baedeker.

.   .   .   .

Constantine Pobedonostev, the lay official who as Procurator of the Holy Synod exercised the Tsar's supreme control over the Russian Orthodox Church, convened a conference of high ecclesiastics in 1891 to consider the spread of the Baptist, Stundist and 'Paschkoff' heresies. Twenty-eight out of the forty-one dioceses were reported seriously infected. The conference resolved that 'the rapid increase of these sects is a serious danger to the State', and petitioned for the sternest measures, from loss of civil rights to the removal of children from parental control.

The policy of the State turned from repression to elimination. Although modified by the endemic inefficiency which always frustrated the intentions of St. Petersburg, the sufferings of Russian-speaking evangelicals in the early eighteen-nineties shocked the conscience of the Western world, as tales filtered through of imprisonments, forced labour, outrages on women, floggings. 'We implore you, beloved brothers, with tears in our eyes,' runs an appeal which reached Quakers in Pennsylvania from the Baptists of Kiev in 1892, 'take this account of ours and give it to somebody who can speak out loudly, and perhaps people will hear us in our most terrible distress.'

Tsarist governments were not wholly indifferent to world opinion; representations from foreign Churches and even from the British Government led to a muting of persecution after the young, ill-fated Nicholas II ascended the throne in 1894. Church and State professed to acknowledge a man's right to believe what he wished, but rejected the right to leave the Orthodox Church or to propagate by mouth or pen 'the views of heretics or dissenters'. Racial minorities in the Empire such as Letts, Poles and Lithuanians were allowed a measure of toleration for their ancestral faith, whether Lutheran or Roman; Russians were not.

Repression continued, until in 1905, following the ferment of the Russo-Japanese War and the abortive revolution which forced the granting of a constitution, the Tsar proclaimed an Act of Toleration, followed by a Manifesto giving freedom of conscience, rights of association and speech, and an amnesty for all who had been imprisoned or exiled for religious crimes.

.   .   .   .

Freedom proved conditional and somewhat precarious, beset by nagging police, irritated priests and the weight of government support for the State Church. Nevertheless, in the nine years between 1905 and the outbreak of the First World War new 'prayer-houses' (as evangelical church buildings were called) rose in many cities and villages, religious magazines began publication from St. Petersburg, where preachers' training courses, illegal hitherto, developed in 1913 to become the first Protestant Bible School in Russia. In the South, where Stundists had now merged with Baptists, Pavlov and Ivanov-Klishnikov, each battered but unspoiled by chain-gang, treadmill and exile, worked hard, the one from Baku, the other from Odessa, to build up a cohesive Baptist Union and instruct country groups whose long years without pastoral leadership had left them more zealous than wise.

The North was dominated by two masterful characters, Ivan Stepanovitch Prokhanov and the young Wilhelm Fettler. Prokhanov came from the Caucasus and had trained as an electrical engineer in order to be self-supporting, 'but at the same time I would serve the Lord with all my power and ability by spreading the Gospel', During the years of repression he had founded an evangelical magazine which had to be printed in Stockholm and smuggled in. He wrote more than 600 hymns and adapted others (not always with acknowledgment), had travelled in America and Europe and spent a year at a Baptist college in England. In 1909 he organized and became first President of the All-Russia Evangelical Christian Union.

Fettler, from Latvia, had also attended an English Baptist college. He was only twenty-four when he settled in St. Petersburg as a pastor, and made an immediate mark as a fluent, magnetic evangelist. He lived as a permanent guest at Princess Lieven's (he used to irk her by inviting people to stay without permission) and opened twelve preaching halls, formed Sunday Schools, inspired the building of the Dom Evangelia or 'House of the Gospel' in St. Petersburg and the church in Moscow which is now famous as the Baptist/Evangelical Christian centre. Prokhanov and Fettler were vital to each other, but each sought exclusive control and wanted all the credit. In later years Fettler, who changed his name to Basil Marlov after emigrating to America, even allowed it to be thought that he had founded the sect of Evangelical Christians, while Prokhanov in his autobiography (published in America in 1933) ignores Fettler's existence.

Whatever their idiosyncrasies the two men had passionate faith and their influence was broad and deep. These years of toleration consolidated and enlarged the evangelical movement. Though too short to affect the course of Russian history, for national reformation had been rejected in the 'eighties and 'nineties and the initiative was passing to atheist extremists, the pre-war decade fashioned the evangelicals into a sizable, vigorous minority with active membership of at least 1,000,000. The strongest areas were still the Ukraine and the Caucasus.

August 1914 ended toleration. The Bible College was forcibly closed, Fettler was sentenced to Siberia, his sentence being commuted to banishment. Prokhanov was indicted but not arrested. Many young Baptists suffered as conscientious objectors. The Evangelical Christians, on the other hand, were not all pacifists. Men who were called to the colours turned barracks into mission

74

fields before disappearing into the mists and miseries of the Polish and Galician fronts where corruption and inefficiency were hastening the suicide of Tsarist Russia.

Some 2,000,000 Russians were taken prisoner. Austrian and German evangelical societies were exhaustive in relief and religious work in the prison camps, one instance among the many in which the calamities of 1914–18, as Prokhanov asserts, 'helped the spreading of the Gospel in a wonderful way'.

And when, in November 1917, the Communists seized power from the liberal revolutionaries who had overthrown Nicholas II in March, the establishment of atheist government had, for Baptists and Evangelical Christians, a most unexpected effect.

CHAPTER IX

RED SURPRISE

FEW evangelicals would have read Lenin's outburst of 1913, 'Every religious idea, every idea of God, even flirting with the idea of God, is unutterable vileness.' They merely knew that Lenin and all Bolsheviks were atheists.

One of the earliest decrees of the new Communist government, issued on January 23rd 1918, though Russia was in chaos and the Germans advancing on Petrograd,[1] separated the Church from the State and the School from the Church and proclaimed, 'Every citizen may adhere to any religion or adhere to none.' Local laws which would 'hinder or limit freedom of conscience' were prohibited. Church and religious societies lost the right to own property, but could have free tenancy of their buildings, now State-owned. Religious teaching, abolished in schools, was permitted privately for the first two years of the new regime until in 1921 religious instruction for any under eighteen, in church or at home, except in groups of three or less, became punishable with one year's imprisonment. Since an additional charge of counter-revolution would normally be incurred, a Sunday School teacher after 1921 could be shot or sent to prison for six years: 'As the Soviet government is responsible for the children of the country it must prevent the minds of children from being darkened by religious superstition.'

Despite this rigorous limitation, the advent of atheist Communism brought the evangelicals a freedom more real than any known under the Tsars.

In the early nineteen-twenties, when civil war, famine and terror ravaged Russia, thousands of evangelical corpses must have lain among the untold million or more who had died by starvation or violence. They died as Russians, not for their faith. When the great persecution began in 1922 which brought upon the Russian

[1] St. Petersburg became Petrograd in 1914, Leningrad in 1924.

76

Orthodox Church fearful retribution for the past and purged it by fire, the evangelicals escaped. They had no hierarchy to be broken, no costly vessels and gilded buildings to be seized. They were known to have been 'subjected to the most cruel persecution on the part of Tsarism', as the Communist Twelfth Party Congress put it in 1923, and essentially were of the 'popular masses', although Party doctrine insisted they must be bourgeois reactionaries at heart.

With Orthodoxy's hold, almost unbreakable before 1917, prised loose by the Revolution the famous piety of the Russian peasant seemed to be vanishing swiftly into a hilarious, boisterous irreligion. Yet a thousand years of Christianity left deep awareness of God, unsated spiritual hunger. For every young man or woman who gloried in the new atheism there were hundreds, young or old, who were dismayed by Communism's contempt for traditional values of justice, honour and truth.

The soul of Russia lay wide open. This was the evangelicals' opportunity. Free not only to believe but to preach and persuade, they advanced rapidly. The two groups, Evangelical Christians and Baptists, often overlapped and a plan of Union was drawn up in 1921 but not signed, partly because Prokhanov did not relish loss of dominance (Fettler had returned to his homeland, Latvia, where he was a major religious figure during its twenty years of independence). They shared the Bible School reopened at Petrograd in 1922, had joint literary activities and relief organizations.

A third force entered the new Soviet Union: the Pentecostalists. The Pentecostal movement had originated a few years previously in America. Though at that time without cohesive organization and little understood by older Churches, it was spreading among the lesser educated and uncultured of all continents, begetting an emotional warmth, a confident faith, zeal and, above all, a 'speaking in tongues' which staid Christian leaders, when they took notice, rejected as delusion, but which Pentecostalists believed to be the Holy Spirit's gift, a primary and long lost feature of the earliest Christians. Also from America but insignificant before 1917 were the Seventh Day Adventists, preaching the Christian Gospel with their own special interpretations and additions. In the moral, spiritual and physical anarchy of early Revolutionary

77

Russia Pentecostalists and Adventists were soon reckoning adherents in thousands. They, the Baptists, the Evangelical Christians and dozens of independent groups with recent or with pre-Revolutionary origin were all termed 'sectarians' by the State.

The early 'twenties brought sectarians their hour—at the very time when evangelical religion in America and Britain lay on the defensive, dismissed as outmoded and impotent.

The freedom allowed them is an aspect of early Soviet rule little remembered outside Russia and carefully expunged from government histories within. Local soviets often gave preachers permits to have notices printed advertising special meetings; the soviet of Tsaritsyn (the future Stalingrad, now Volgograd) allowed the Baptist pastor free use of the city theatre for his Sunday services; when the Kazan soviet closed the evangelical prayer-house Lenin himself intervened. Russian believers like to think that had Lenin lived their fate would have been different and they may be right—for all his diatribes against religion and his ruthlessness.

Sectarian leaders were not without dangers and difficulties. The pacifism that some of them professed and taught led to collisions with the authorities until the Baptist Union agreed to allow its youth to serve in the Red Army. Prokhanov was twice imprisoned on charges of counter-revolution. At Tver (now Kalinin) in 1921 he and his entire Young People's Conference were locked up. They continued their sessions in prisons, praying, reading the Bible, singing hymns so lustily that the Cheka[1] chief complained: 'We have had all kinds of prisoners here, but we have never had such noisy fellows as you are! You sing all the time. You disturb us in our work. The people gather in the streets around the building. We cannot allow you to continue this noise any longer!' The Youth Conference argued that if they could not sing at liberty, 'We must have the right to sing in prison.' As a compromise they were permitted to sing and pray two hours in the morning, two in the evening.

Such a conversation and so generous a compromise were to become unthinkable a few years later.

.   .   .   .

[1] The Secret or Security Police has had various designations at different stages of Soviet history: Cheka, G.P.U., N.K.V.D., M.V.D., K.G.B.

The League of Militant Godless, founded in 1925 by the Communist Party, for 'active, systematic and continuous struggle against religion in all its forms and appearances', strove to overthrow the greatest evil they knew.

They used mockery and propaganda, gave lectures, made house-to-house visits. They caused the closing of many Moscow churches. In the provinces, however, their public debates sometimes had the reverse effect. The lecturer's normal weapon was a naïve use of a few Bible verses out of context to demonstrate the futility or dishonesty of religion: most of the audience revered their Bibles but barely knew them and would be impressed by the show of authority. If, however, an evangelical were present it was a simple matter to confound the atheist by putting his verses back into context, asking him questions which revealed his scanty knowledge of Scripture and capping him by genuine Bible teaching. This the people greeted with applause, and according to Prokhanov, the debates often led to 'new hearers filling our meetings'.

In country districts a pair of Godless propagandists would descend on a village. Within a week or two the people would vote to expel the priest and turn the church into a club. The Godless then pass on happily to the next village. Within a month an evangelist wanders in, and when the atheists come round again they would discover to their horror most of the village lustily singing Baptist hymns in the 'club'. Maurice Hindus, a young Russian-born American journalist whose fluency in his mother tongue enabled him to travel widely in the Soviet Union in the 'twenties, heard one of these roving evangelists preaching at a country fair in Belorussia. 'He was a giant of a man, with a downy reddish beard . . . He had a bony, ascetic face, which only accentuated the flaming brilliance of his large blue eyes . . . He had come from somewhere in the south. He was wandering from village to village, covering as many fairs as he could and always repeating the same speech.'

The man was probably an independent. The accredited representatives of the Baptist and the Evangelical Christian Unions found equal response: 'Brother Ivan Stepanovitch,' Prokhanov would read in a hasty note from one of his missionaries, 'I am a captive of the Gospel. They take me from one village to another and I do not know where I will stop or when I will be able to return.' Nor were the industrial proletariat deaf to a vigorous Christian message. And with a rising standard of literacy in the new State there was demand for Bibles. Most Russian families before the Revolution possessed at least a New Testament, but many Bibles had been torn up for cigarette paper during the Civil War. Lack of funds was the only ban to a fresh printing. Prokhanov went to America, raised money, and the Evangelical Christians put out editions of 35,000 Bibles and 25,000 New Testaments in 1926–28, printed on atheist government presses.

International aid. Freedom to print, to travel and preach. A new Baptist Preachers' School in Moscow. A missionary society founded in 1927 as 'Friends of the Mission among Heathen and Mohammedans', which sent out seven specially trained evangelists. All these reflect the comparative freedom of religion before Stalin reached supremacy—a freedom so forgotten that when I asked Baptist leaders of the 'sixties about their Mission to the Heathen and Mohammedans in the 'twenties they could not believe it had ever existed.

.   .   .   .

In the land mass of the Soviet Union, with its scattered population of 150,000,000, evangelicals by 1927 numbered at most 2,000,000, many of whom were congregated in certain areas. While village after village had never seen a Baptist, the movement was spreading at speed.

Perhaps—it is not an excessive claim—the evangelicals were the key to Russia's happiness. For in Communist theory, mixed up with the violence and hatred lay a passionate idealism which sought to remake a nation; Lenin and the early Soviet Communists fervently desired the welfare of all mankind, but were chained by false views of how to attain it. The evangelicals had this same desire, and by the beauty of their lives demonstrated the moral virtues which the atheists only professed. Maurice Hindus, of Jewish faith himself, always asked for a Baptist house when he reached a village, 'knowing that I would live in a clean house, in a tranquil family atmosphere, where the man would defer to his wife with a sense of chivalry that was as new as it was refreshing in Russian peasant society'. Evangelicals were winning a reputation for agricultural work and had even set up communal farms on the very model that was soon to be imposed by force throughout Russia without the motive of mutual love. Some of them received State grants, and many were officially praised for their efficiency. One of the early Communist leaders publicly described them as the economic and cultural vanguard in the countryside.

Unfortunately, the prospect of their wider influence on the new nation was ruined by the fact that atheism is written into Communism. By the Party line therefore sectarians were a foul infection in the body of the State. 'The Party cannot be neutral in regard to religion,' Stalin said in 1927.

The Party was already alarmed by the progress of religion. 'The clergy and the sectarians are carrying on a wild propaganda,' stated *Pravda* in April 1928. 'It would be useless to imagine that only old women and old men go to church. Hundreds of thousands of young workmen can be found in churches and in the sectarian prayer-houses.' A leader of the Militant Godless complained in November 1928 that in the Melitopol district of the Ukraine about ninety per cent of the youth was under the influence of the Baptists' young men's association, and *Komsomolskaya Pravda*, daily organ of the Komsomol, was disgusted to discover that the 'numerous sectarian organizations unite about the same number of members as the Komsomol does . . . The growing generation is being submerged by the murky waves of religion.'

A short while later the Commissar of Education, Lunacharsky, called on the Party to mobilize for 'the repulse of the religious danger . . . I should like in the most sadistic manner to root out and tear out this utter weed from our fields and gardens.'

CHAPTER X

STALIN'S WINTERS

In the summer of 1928 the Congress of the Baptist World Alliance in Toronto heard the Reverend P. B. Ivanov-Klishnikov, Principal of the Baptist Preachers' School in Moscow and son of the pioneer, give such a glowing account of Soviet liberality to evangelicals that many of his Western hearers were affronted. Bred on tales, only too true, of Soviet attacks on Orthodox and Roman Catholic clergy and justifiably uneasy at Russian propaganda for world revolution, they could not stomach Ivanov's compliments to the regime. In London he repeated his optimistic forecast. 'We look for the steady progress of the churches,' he told the *Baptist Times*.

His optimism was quickly exploded. On return to Moscow Ivanov was arrested and exiled to Central Asia. The Preachers' School at Moscow and the Bible School at Leningrad were closed. Christian magazines were ordered to reduce circulation by ninety per cent and afterwards forbidden publication. On April 8th 1929 were revoked the Law of 1918 which permitted freedom of religion and the even more liberal decree of June 1928, short-lived and soon forgotten, which permitted the erection of new prayer-houses without any hindrance and forbade the closing of prayer-houses by local soviets except for serious reasons. In their place the new Law of 1929 sharply reduced the rights of all believers, stopped preachers travelling from district to district and broke up those subsidiary groups which had been a sectarian feature: happy little sewing circles, which for many women had been an introduction to the Baptist Church, were dissolved. Young men and women arriving for the week-night meeting of Christomol or Baptomol were sadly told by the pastor that Komsomol was now the only legal youth organization in the U.S.S.R. Literacy classes and Bible classes were banned. A Church or a sect might gather for no other purpose than a normal service of worship, with or without sermon.

The most bitter blow lay in the abolition of freedom for religious propaganda while retaining freedom of worship. The relevant clause in the Constitution henceforth read: 'Freedom of religious worship and freedom of *anti-religious* propaganda is recognized for all citizens.'[1] At a stroke, religious propaganda became illegal. The giant young man with downy reddish beard whom Hindus heard preach at the country fair would be clapped in jail. At atheist lectures no evangelical could again lift his voice, no poster advertising an evangelistic rally could be seen on the streets and the rally itself would be unlawful. Nine of the ten evangelical churches in Leningrad were forcibly closed, three of the four in Moscow. Orthodox and sectarian places of worship that remained were targets for Komsomol hooligans, who frequently broke up services and beat up worshippers. Presbyters were taken away for questioning. Sherwood Eddy, the American Student Christian Movement leader, was shocked to find his Baptist girl interpreter coughing blood. 'She had been cruelly struck by a raging atheist ex-priest in the torture chamber of the G.P.U. until her lungs bled freely.'

The Baptists and Evangelical Christians were now the special targets of the Soviet State.

They were attacked for their foreign connections. The money raised in America, an example of Christian aid crossing rigid political fences, became bribery by international bourgeoisie and capitalist crooks; the visits abroad of Ivanov and Prokhanov (who was out of Russia when the persecution began, and never returned), which had helped towards removing Western suspicion of the revolutionary regime, became sinister conspiracies to counter-revolution. As if to give substance to such allegations, a 'band of Baptist spies' was put on trial in Minsk in February 1929: twenty-five people who had been trained at a Baptist institute in America were charged with settling in Belorussia in order to carry on espionage. In the Ukraine a prominent Baptist was even arraigned as a spy of the Polish General Staff.

They were accused of economic sabotage. The religious co-operative farms so praised a few years earlier as patterns of 'Communist principles in agriculture' were liquidated (though a

[1] Italics mine.

few seem to have survived until the war) or forcibly absorbed into atheist communes. In the great Collectivization which wrought such suffering and led to the Famine of 1929–31, sectarian farmers—hard working and therefore prosperous—were inevitably classed as *kulaks*, though the word had originally meant 'tight-fisted'. Most were shot or deported.

Stalin treated clergy of all faiths as third-class citizens, without voting rights, kept to a severely reduced bread ration and subject to penal taxation. Sectarian preachers who were laymen in trades missed the first force of discriminatory laws, until submerged by the flood of accusation and defamation pouring from the Party-controlled Press and hooked upon one technicality or another.

No Tsarist persecution could compare with the exquisite Soviet combination of mental and physical brutality. The experience of an evangelical clergyman from a German colony in the Ukraine was that of countless Baptists: 'During the latter days of my twenty-two days and twenty-two nights without sleep I was made to stand for four and a half hours, sit for half an hour and then stand again.' At intervals he was cross-examined for hours on end, his interrogator swearing and screaming, sometimes wheedling and promising, in a last effort to extract a false confession. Despite increasing spasms of near-insanity, the clergyman stood his ground: 'I know only one way, and that is the way of truth. If it leads me to the abyss, so be it. I refused to turn aside. Death in this place is not the worst that can happen to me. The worst would come after death if I were disloyal to my faith.'

.   .   .   .

The sufferings of active Christians were absorbed into the wider tragedy of the Great Purges of the 'thirties. A vast slave army of between 7,000,000 and 14,000,000 Soviet citizens toiled in Arctic timber camps or the coalfields of Karaganda, on construction of the White Sea Canal or in the uranium mines.

The overcrowded cells of remand prisons saw countless acts of charity, heard countless words of consolation, in the name of Jesus Christ. The inhumanly long hours of the slave labour camps, the relentless demands of the work 'norm' that must be fulfilled in agonizing cold on starvation rations formed the school of Christian service from which graduated many of the present leaders of Russian evangelical churches. They seldom speak of it, even since Khrushchev brought into the open the grim story of the Purges; indeed, they will say gallantly that they did not suffer as much as other sectors of the population.

The slave camps were schools of Christian unity. Orthodox, Baptists, Roman Catholics, German Mennonites, all receiving the worst treatment, the hardest spheres of labour, the constant taunt of 'You devilish priests!' learned to respect and love one another as fellow-sufferers for Christ. Barriers between sectarians and Orthodox which had been thrown high by one persecution began to break down in another.

.   .   .   .

By 1937 a generation was reaching maturity which had never heard religious teaching at school, but had been bred instead to atheism. Nevertheless, in the census of 1937 one-third of the entire population in towns, two-thirds in rural areas, stated they were Believers, which implied active belief, since any who rejected the label 'Atheist' might list themselves 'Indifferent or Undecided'. The total census figures revealed that in the Soviet Union there were more declared Christians than any other category, a fact which so shocked the government that no census has ever again put questions on religious affiliation.

The German invasion and the bitter battles and losses of the 'Great Patriotic War' forced even Stalin to acknowledge Russia's need for her Churches.

He restored the Patriarchate and suppressed the League of Militant Godless. Sectarians received recognition too. The union of Baptists and Evangelical Christians, which might have come earlier had not the Great Purge supervened, was achieved in 1944–45. The State required it, the leaders of both evangelical groups welcomed it. The two great wings, together with a proportion of the Pentecostalists, fused under the leadership of the *All-Union Council of Evangelical Christians/Baptists*. The adherents of the Union have generally been known since by the short title of *Baptists*.

A considerable number of Evangelical Christians, Baptists and

85

Pentecostalists refused to affiliate with the new Council. This independence, whether right or wrong or half right, maintains a tension in the nineteen-sixties which is of such importance to the whole contemporary situation, and to the story of the Thirty Two Siberians, that it must be examined fully in a later chapter.

The All-Union leaders paid a price for recognition and toleration. Those statements on Stalin's 'peace campaign', or 'Imperialism', 'American germ warfare', etc., and on Hungary, which sounded strange on Christian lips to those who knew the truth about Korea or the events of 1956, were believed by Western Baptists to be a part of the price.

Formation of the All-Union Council in 1944–45 brought a second spring to the evangelical movement. And this spring continued to flower in Stalin's second icy winter of repression. Baptist growth in the early Soviet period is no more surprising than Baptist decline during the Purges and recovery under wartime toleration. By the same token there should have been a falling off by the early 'fifties. Yet the number of adult baptisms and of new communities rose with each year of a persecution which, if less violent than before, sent thousands of pastors, laymen and laywomen to the penal labour camps, especially from the newly swallowed Baltic states and Polish provinces, and from Russian territory recovered from the Germans. Most never expected to see home again.

In Solzhenitsyn's novel, *One Day in the Life of Ivan Denisovich*, the character Aloysha, the Baptist from the Caucasus doing a stretch of twenty-five years, has copied out the forbidden New Testament into a notebook, and urges Shukhov (Solzhenitsyn himself) to pray. 'For my part,' he quotes from the Apostle Paul, 'I am ready not merely to be bound but even to die for the name of the Lord Jesus.' John Noble, a young American who served four years of hard labour in the frozen inferno of Vorkuta (1950–54) is even more explicit: 'The Baptists were making converts among groups of all nationalities.' Despite the fearful punishment received by a clergyman of any church who was caught conducting a service in the camp, the Baptists had found a way of holding Bible sessions in the mess-hall.

'While we were eating,' writes Noble, 'a group would gather at

86

one of the corner tables in the back of dining area, and among them one or two men would engage in seemingly casual conversation. Only when you drew near and sat down with your tin plate of salt fish and black bread, would you realize that what they were talking about was a passage from the Bible. Everyone else would sit quietly eating while these leaders discussed some Bible story or commented on the teachings of Christ in their necessarily casual way. We had no Bibles, but, since these men knew their Scriptures by heart, we could get along without them.' If a newcomer to the barracks showed interest they would invite him to join them. Many were from districts where every church had been closed for years, and were shy of a forbidden religious meeting; 'when they discovered what nourishment the Lord had waiting for them there, they thirsted for more than casual talk and before long were regular attendants'.

When Stalin died in March 1953 the Baptists had shown adversity to be no enemy.

.   .   .   .

With other former 'enemies of the people' the majority of imprisoned Christians were released in the opening of the camps during the three years following Stalin's death.

The return of pastors from exile, the re-opening of prayer-houses and the other signs of the slow thaw felt throughout the Soviet Union were accompanied at first by a renewed campaign of vilification against all things and men religious, until November 11th 1954. On that day, signed by Nikita Sergeyevich Khrushchev as First Secretary, the Central Committee of the Party issued its famous Decree, *On Mistakes in the Conduct of Scientific-Atheist Propaganda among the Population*.

The Decree admitted 'gross errors'. Newspapers were criticized for 'insulting attacks' on clergy and believers, for depicting them as 'people unworthy of political trust'. Party officials were rebuked for administrative interference in 'the activity of religious associations and groups, and also of a rough attitude towards the clergy'. 'The Party has always considered it necessary,' stated the Decree with strict regard to theory if strict abuse of facts, 'to avoid offending the feelings of believers in any way.'

This was the core of the new approach. Errors in propaganda and local administration had done serious harm to the anti-religious campaign. All Party organizations were 'not in any event to permit in future any offence to the feelings of believers or Church ministers or administrative interference in the activity of the Churches'.

.   .   .   .

A decade has passed since Mr. Khrushchev signed the Decree of 1954.

Part One of this book has shown that, despite it, 'offence to the feelings of believers' is permitted today. Part Three must sift evidence of 'administrative interference in the activity of Churches', and evidence of other external pressures.

To do this it is essential first to plunge deep into the present daily life of these Christians who have not only survived but thrived under the worst that Tsar or Party could inflict.

PART THREE

CONFLICT

CHAPTER XI

THE CITADEL

SCARCELY a city in the U.S.S.R. now lacks a Baptist prayer-house. Baptists are strong in the Baltic and Western lands which were not Soviet before the war, well spread in villages and cities of the Ukraine, in parts of Central Russia and the Caucasus. Central Asia, with its hybrid population of European immigrants living among indigenous Moslems, has city congregations of 900, 1,000, 1,200 and more; Baptists are expanding in Western Siberia and the Soviet Far East.

The Baptists of the U.S.S.R. are more numerous than those of any Baptist Church outside the United States. The fifteen-man All-Union Council of Evangelical Christians/Baptists has oversight of about 5,500 congregations.[1] These congregations are supervised by seventy Senior Presbyters, equivalent to bishops at least, who travel throughout their territories by plane or train merely carrying the passport (identity card) required by any citizen before he may move around from his domicile. In October 1963 many Senior Presbyters and other leading pastors and laymen, over 400 from all over the nation, gathered at Moscow for a three-day Congress, the first since the Unity Conference of 1944, in the evangelical church in the Maly Vuzovsky sidestreet not far from Red Square. Foreigners frequently visit this, the single Evangelical/Baptist church in Moscow. The crowded pews, aisles and galleries, the superb choir and reverent service provide an authentic sight—despite the claim by a few Westerners that congregation, choir and preachers form a Communist 'front' of hypocrites well drilled to deceive tourists. Nevertheless, for the purest flavour of their essence the visitor must join Baptists far from Moscow.

[1] The figures given by the All-Union Council in the application for membership of the World Council of Churches in 1962 were: 545,000 members, 5,545 churches, 5,545 pastors, 32,270 preachers.

The first impression will be of a plain box-like building, well kept, with illuminated texts on the walls. A text sure to be found is: *Bog est Lyubov* (God is Love). A platform holds choir, pastor's reading desk and seats for special guests; the Communion Table is often simply the officiating pastor's table specially prepared on a Sacrament Sunday. John Lawrence describes one of the congregations with which he worshipped: 'Before us, on the right, sat men with long beards looking just like illustrations from Tolstoy; younger men sat behind. On the left sat a wonderful collection of grandmothers with strong, ugly faces; behind them were the younger women, all wearing head-scarves. Every face was intent and we could see tears rolling down. Every Russian Baptist congregation is the same and each one is different. They always look like a scene from Hogarth transfigured. These are people who have lived through hard times. There is no lukewarmness. In the Soviet Union either you have transforming faith or you do not have faith at all.'

The service on Sundays, and that at mid-week which is almost as largely attended, is simple, unliturgical yet dignified and carrying unconscious hints of the Orthodox tradition in which the early Russian Baptists were bred. The same sense of being part of a mighty stream of Christian life is seen in the custom of greetings: a visitor brings greetings from his home church, which the entire congregation will immediately return by rising to shout in unison: 'Greetings to ——.' At the close of a service visitors are always dismissed with *God be with you till we meet again*, adapted to an inimitable chant-like tempo; there was considerable surprise on learning that words and tune had American originals.

The prayer during service further strengthens the feelings of being one family. The pastor leads aloud, extempore, and the congregation join him audibly: he puts a petition which each person echoes in his or her words until the church is filled with a whispering like a quiet sea lapping celestial sands. I have met it once before, in Borneo, where in a Christian longhouse they gather together at dawn, each whispering individual devotions yet heartened by his neighbour. In Russia after the pastor's prayer two or three of the congregation will follow with brief spontaneous thanksgivings or petitions.

A most memorable feature is the singing.

Every church has its choir of young men and women and a few older folk. Undoubtedly this singing, in a music-loving nation, is a road by which outsiders come into the church. A choir practice is technically illegal but normally unhindered by local authorities— an instance of that compromise which in fact runs throughout the State's handling of religion and is in itself a condemnation of policy: laws usually violated lest life be intolerable are bad laws. And they may always be invoked by the ill-disposed; a sword hangs over the heads of believers.

The singing is generally unaccompanied. Every choir leader has a tuning fork and conducts. The marvellous Russian sense of pitch and time permits complicated harmonies and changes of tempo, though congregational hymns are sung slowly in Orthodox tradition and the scarcity of hymn-books is offset by the pastor reading out each verse before it is sung. Anthems are written on manuscript paper, new hymns or versions being passed and adapted from church to church, anonymous, unsophisticated, as true and distinctive folk music as the negro spiritual.

The hymns are based on Scripture. Words and tune so express the faith of the people, their aspirations, experience and suffering as to disclose the very heart of this vigorous movement in modern Russia. Even in prose translation without music the words have power and pathos.

One of the best loved is *Khochu lyubit silney* (I want to love more strongly), based on 1 John 4:19: 'We love Him because He first loved us':

Hear my prayer and the sighing of my spirit, my God,
I want to love Thee more strongly.
I want to love with the fire of sacred prayer,
With all my heart and mind and all my soul.

In vain I sought peace in the darkness of the world's busyness,
Only Thy testament of love gave me peace,
If ever I see the threat of tribulation,
Just then I want to love more strongly.

When my life is cut off for the days of eternity,
Even in Heaven I want to love more strongly.
And I know that I shall be where there are no shadows,
Where God's eternal temple is, to love more strongly.

Many hymns are written round the theme of the Cross, such as this for solo and chorus:

Praise be to the holy love of the Father,
Who sent Christ into the world to suffer!
And in the tortures of the Cross
He drank the whole cup to the dregs.

Chorus.   *Only by the power of Christ*
Are all our fetters taken off.
God has done so much for us!
Praise be to the love of Christ!

And here is the first verse of a rousing solo and chorus on conflict and victory, a sort of Russian *Stand up! Stand up for Jesus!*

We will stand firm for the Gospel faith, for Christ;
Following His example, forward all, forward after Him!

Chorus.   *In a friendly, joyful family,*
As His one people.
With one heart and soul,
Forward after Christ, forward! [1]

.   .   .   .

The core of the service is the preaching. The service lasts about two hours and contains at least two sermons, strong Biblical sermons in which Scriptural teaching is expounded in depth and breadth, and the congregation visibly (sometimes audibly) takes the preacher's points. Speaker and listeners are soaked in the

[1] These hymns are translated by John W. Lawrence from the Russian Baptist Hymn-book.

94

Bible: Scripture illuminates Scripture, allusions are caught instantly, thoughts may be followed through without involved explanations. Unconsciously it is Wesley and Spurgeon and Moody rolled into one, yet distinctively Russian; it is traditional yet contemporary, an amalgam of Biblical doctrine and stark experience.

The standard of sermons must vary because preaching, together with part-time pastoral work, is the only theological training of almost all embryo ministers; a Preacher's School is still a hope unfulfilled, and though six young men spent two years at British Baptist colleges in the later nineteen-fifties they have not been followed by others. Lack of theological education is offset by the tradition that sermons must be true to the Bible. The Russian examines what the New Testament teaches about man and God, sets it in the unfolding context of the whole Bible as a unity, and proclaims it. For him the Bible as received is the revealed Word of God, to be proclaimed: and he believes unquestioningly that the Holy Spirit applies His Word to the minds and hearts of the sincere. The Bible speaks to his condition, makes sense. He seeks to live by it, but seems free of mechanical text-throwing or text-tearing; probably because to him the Risen Christ, 'the Lord', is his nearest Friend and 'the Word' is no jumble of formulae but the means by which the Lord teaches, an inexhaustible mine of wisdom.[1]

This hunger for 'the Word' is a distinctive feature of Russian Baptists. 'When I visit a church,' says a Senior Presbyter, 'after the service some of them will sit up all night, perhaps, asking me questions, problems of behaviour, problems of the Word: "What does this verse mean?" "What does that verse mean?" Their mouths are wide open, panting, hungry for the Word. They lap it up.'

This makes the shortage of Bibles the more poignant. 'There

[1] Attempts to reinterpret Christianity for 'man come of age', in the manner of Bishop Robinson's *Honest to God*, which was much discussed in Moscow after a B.B.C. broadcast, would seem to them irrelevant to the Russian facts of life. (A Party member and atheist, an official of the Council for Religious Cults, said to us: 'I hear one of your bishops has proved there is no God!')

95

was apparent a great need in our communities of Bibles, New Testaments and Hymn-books,' wrote the chairman of the All-Union Council after a visit to western Siberia early in 1963, 'but we hope that the Lord will allow this need of our churches to be satisfied.'

Urgent requests are received by Christian broadcasting stations which offer to mail Russian Bibles, and for every listener who writes, scores must consider it wiser to refrain.

'Dear Sir, Not long ago we bought a radio set,' writes a man who may not himself be a believer, to the Far East Broadcasting Company, of Manila,[1] 'and every evening all of us are listening to different programmes of foreign countries. Very often we are listening to the programme "The Voice of the East" from the Philippines. Our grandmother likes very much your programme. They are coming through very clearly. She would like very much to have the Bible (The Old Testament) and other religious literature, and she is asking you to send her everything that is possible. With great impatience she expects your letter and in advance expresses her gratitude.' A woman was astonished to hear over the air an apparent echo from her own prayer-house; her letter is an eloquent commentary on Soviet broadcasting policy. 'I greet you with the love of our Lord Jesus Christ,' she wrote in May 1963. 'I received your programme over the Radio and I was so surprised that our Brothers and Sisters can preach over the Radio the Word of God. I never thought that our Pentecostals would preach over the Radio . . . A hearty greeting from all of us, may the Lord bless you for your Labour in His work. Pray for us, and we will pray for you.'

Letters bring pressing requests: 'We beg of you to send us God's Book because it is impossible to get it here' . . . 'Dear Brother, I badly need literature in Russian language, the Bible' . . . 'Brothers and sisters, I have a request to make: if possible send me a Bible, I ask for this Grace of the Lord, don't refuse it to me because here I have no opportunity to obtain one' . . . And an industrial toiler deep in Central Asia, a man called Peter who evidently is not in touch with any church, ends a muddled letter with the plea: 'I could write much more, but I don't have a Bible . . . You also

[1] These and other letters are given in literal translation made by F.E.B.C.

offer to send a Bible; I have a great need. Will be grateful to you wholeheartedly.'

.   .   .   .

The Baptist communities have the human weaknesses, problems, temptations experienced by Christians anywhere in the world, but the Russian Baptist's faith is his absorbing passion. Life centres round his church. Its fellowship is the citadel from which he can operate in a harsh environment.

He has strong moral discipline. A man may not be ordained presbyter until he is married, and whereas in the Orthodox Church an unmarried man cannot be ordained for a parish ministry but if widowed must not remarry, a Baptist pastor whose wife dies must marry again, unless very old. Sex is possibly a recurrent problem in the churches, for surprise was expressed at the information that many British and American missionaries are unmarried yet that trouble is rare. Extra sensitivity about sex may partly be reaction against early Soviet licence; in the nineteen-twenties abortion, divorce, contraception and pre-marital intercourse were correct revolutionary behaviour.

Some Baptists have an acute distaste for anything smacking of 'worldliness'. Little irritates the Communists more than refusal to frequent cinemas, theatres and dances; and the contempt, where it is found, for art and culture. Baptists in the great cities are by no means uncultured. 'Some of our country members are very narrow minded,' they will say, 'very conservative. Some won't take a plane. Some of the pastors won't even use a bicycle because of the old tradition that "the Lord's work should be done on foot".' One pastor was quietly amused when a pale-faced youth in his flock expressed astonishment at a suggestion he take up a sport. The youth quoted St. Paul, 'Bodily exercise profits little', etc. The pastor explained the true meaning of the text and sent him off to do gymnastics.

The Biblical injunction is accepted strictly: 'Love not the world, neither the things that are in the world. If any man love the world, the love of the Father is not in him. For all that is in the world, the lust of the flesh, and the lust of the eyes, and the pride of life, is not of the Father but is of the world.' The 'world' is interpreted from a Puritan viewpoint underlined by the traditional emphasis of Old Believers (the cultural background from which many early Baptists sprang) on being unpolluted. Unworldliness is a strong cohesive element, as it was for nineteenth-century evangelicals in England and America, a line of defence and demarcation. It may run to extremes, despite Baptist leaders' attempts to prevent this. But were the Soviet way of life less deliberately hostile, were the frontier between belief and unbelief less rigidly walled, wired and mined by Communism's hatred of Christianity the extremes would be gently eased away.

The Baptists look more for what a man is than what he does, to his personal character rather than his taste in amusements. Serious infringement of the moral code is swiftly judged by exclusion from Holy Communion or from fellowship. Dancing or playgoing would not probably be denounced except in remote country districts, but a member caught drinking liquor will be warned; if caught frequently he will be suspended. Sexual immorality would lead to expulsion. Most of the backsliders whose shocking revelations of Baptist wickedness are printed in atheist pamphlets are black sheep of this sort. A younger pastor said to Maurice Hindus, 'Baptists too can go wrong and betray their faith in their everyday life. As soon as we learn of it we expel them. Then they say terrible things about us. But it doesn't disturb us. We are careful about the citizens who apply for membership. They are on probation for two or three years before they are accepted into the Church.'

Determination to keep 'unspotted from the world' can undoubtedly tend to pharisaism. The price of discipline, in Russia as in any country, is the temptation to judge, to nag, to be self-righteous; churches may be spoiled, growth frustrated. But a sure sign of basic spiritual health among Russian Baptists is that the quality of mercy overrides censoriousness, the positive joys of living outweigh differences about behaviour, fraternal love is no mere catchword; theirs essentially is a New Testament church impregnated by the motto, 'God is Love'. From mutual experience of human frailty and Divine redemption grows unity.

This unity transcends race. The Soviet Government, despite bright posters of grinning citizens grouped in varied national dress, has suffered over the years much trouble with racial minorities reluctant to be assimilated. The Baptist Church has been a powerful if unacknowledged racial synthesizer. In the Virgin Lands and other areas of widespread immigration or deportation the churches may have three or four, in one city no less than eleven different races in Christian amity, the majority being of European origin. In territories having Asian populations alongside the Russian minority the Baptists are conscious of missionary responsibility. Here and there a former Moslem has become a church member. In one city a group of Moslems, distant from the one mosque still open but near the Baptist church, asked their mullah if they might attend. He replied: 'Certainly. They believe in one God, and they don't worship idols like the Orthodox!'

Between Baptist and Orthodox themselves the old suspicions, already resolved at higher levels, are everywhere now dying. A jovial Orthodox Archbishop said of the Baptists, 'They can go where we with our robes and paraphernalia cannot. Our priests can't go into factories. The Baptists can—they work there.' He added, with expressive gestures, 'We used to chase them with a pitchfork. Now we draw them to us with a kiss of peace.'

.   .   .   .

Assumption that Baptists in the U.S.S.R. are hanging on by the finger-nails is quickly disproved. If Paul's phrase 'exceeding joyful in all our tribulation' is exemplified anywhere in the modern world it is in Soviet Russia. They accept difficulties and distresses as the normal lot of a New Testament Christian. Indeed, they go further: 'We are grateful to our government,' they will say, 'for putting us in a position where it costs so much to be a Christian. We thank God for the privilege of living in a land of clear-cut faith. Everybody knows who is a Christian. There used to be so many shades of loyalty and faith; nowadays you have to stand right out or not at all.'

This joy in tribulation is not negative endurance but by-product of joy in God. The Apostle's call, 'Rejoice in the Lord alway: and again I say, rejoice,' reflects the dominant experience: they rejoice 'in the *Lord*'. They have unshakable conviction that the Creator reigns, the Saviour lives. The words of the Second Psalm, which

99

to a Westerner may be no more than archaic imagery or the libretto of one of Handel's most exciting arias, strike them as apt: 'Why do the heathen rage, and the people imagine a vain thing? . . . The rulers take counsel together against the Lord and against His anointed, saying, Let us break their bands asunder, and cast away their cords from us. He that sitteth in the heavens shall laugh: the Lord shall have them in derision.'

To them Christ is more real than the words and acts of those who oppose Him. The Pauline claim, 'Christ liveth in me,' and Christ's promise, 'Lo, I am with you alway' are woven into the very texture of their lives. They walk with the Lord. At a meal with leading laymen in one distant city I asked if church members really did have consciousness of His presence at the workbench, in recreation, in times of difficulty and of happiness. Back came the instant answer, from a great fat middle-aged man, a skilled technologist: 'Elementary. It is the first lesson we learn.'

This tremendous sense of Presence is a primary reason why the citadel is so strong, why atheist propaganda leaves Baptists unscathed. Atheist slander washes harmlessly off the shield of a good conscience, atheist theory bears little relation to truth as Christians see it. There is no conflict between the achievements of Soviet science, in which they rejoice, and the demands of faith. Science cannot save the whole man. 'The way of the Lord is not mechanized,' they put it quaintly. 'Salvation is a *walk*.'

Baptists know perfectly well that the Christian way will never perish from the earth, that they serve the side that will be victorious at the last. Weaker brethren may indeed forget this and fall. A senior presbyter visiting some church in his 'diocese' will often be asked to adjudicate on one who has slipped, or denied his Master. A presbyter said, 'They get teased at their work'—that word 'teased' can be euphemism for stronger pressure.

The brothers and sisters sigh sometimes for better times. Once again Paul has the phrase for it: 'As sorrowful, yet always rejoicing.' The Baptist outlook has developed emphases similar to those that were found among Southern negroes in slavery. The Second Advent of Christ to establish His reign of peace, justice and love is a doctrine dear to them, and Heaven a vivid certainty, where God shall wipe away all tears from their eyes, and there shall be no more death, neither sorrow, nor crying, neither shall there be any more pain.

They are assured when they say farewell with a kiss, in the Russian Christian way, that they will meet again, will 'meet at Jesus' feet', because they do not rely on good deeds but on Him. The Russian Baptist in the midst of an alien world has a glorious assurance freeing him from fear, releasing him for service.

CHAPTER XII

ADVANCE FROM STRENGTH

FROM the citadel of faith and fellowship the Baptists carry their message into 'Soviet reality' (as the Party phrase is) and carry it primarily by transparent goodness of character and action.

At one airport (not where the Intourist girl said Baptists killed people) we arrived late at night, welcomed by an informal committee who during the long wait for Intourist's car sat with us in the lounge, one of them being a retired presbyter with ramrod back, merry eyes and a very delightful smile. Two or three of the airport's clerical staff worked at desks, and when at last we were called to the car and I hurried thankfully towards the door I noticed that old man quietly going round to each saying a cheery good night. The airport clerks had no idea who he was, but their faces lit up. His little act of courtesy shamed me.

It was not an isolated act. The Baptists seemed to shed a touch of light wherever they went. John Lawrence describes a professional man whom we met: 'Youngish, rather ugly, very friendly, he gets inside people's defences in two minutes. The servants at our hotel adore him, though they have only seen him once or twice. He makes a joke out of everything and then speaks very seriously about something serious.'

Atheist slanders fall flat where Baptists are known personally. On November 20th 1963 after a scurrilous attack on a Moldavian presbyter by *Sovetskaya Moldaviya*, a worker at the Kishinev locomotive depot, Aleksandr Chechko, protested to the editors. 'I have been living with him for eight years now and am married to his daughter. My wife and I are unbelievers and at work we are shock-workers of Communist Labour', but he was 'highly indignant when I saw the name of Rudenko G. A., about whom such dirt was being written.'[1] Maurice Hindus in 1960 overheard a

---

[1] The newspaper, of course, only quoted the letter in order to rebuke young Chechko, shock-worker and Party Candidate as he was, for his scandalous defence of one 'hostile to our society'.

young Cossack woman who was selling melons tell a customer in the market-place of Krasnodar: 'When you marry a Baptist you know that he isn't going to stink up the house with the smoke of *makhorka* [cheap tobacco]. You know he isn't going to come home drunk and foul up the house with dirty language, and you know he isn't going to be charmed by another woman.'

Baptists carry their message too by an impeccable integrity most uncharacteristic of Soviet reality, and by trustworthy labour in factory or field, having the advantage over many in a Communist state of satisfying motive: they work for the honour of God. In a typically virulent article on September 5th 1963 *Gudok* attempted to dismiss Baptist emphasis on labour (which it claimed quite inaccurately was a recent development), as 'pious fraud . . . hypocritical tactic of deceit'. 'Soviet people work selflessly for society,' the writer asserted, 'in the name of the building of Communism in our country. Such labour brings joy and deep internal satisfaction.' If he was honest he would admit how often it does not. In Feodov Abramov's recent novel about life on a collective-farm the toilers find every excuse to refuse an extra work day to get in the hay until the chairman, in his cups, promises an extra large percentage for themselves.

The increase of consumer goods now brings more to work for. The Russian has a genius for making the most of any situation, and for creating a private world within a world; but beneath the slogans, the endless exhortations, Soviet man's labour for the State is drab, even in a city where he may go to the circus or puppet theatre, and despite the wonderful material bliss promised for the distant future. The Baptists have a closer incentive. The apt words of the Apostle Peter are taken literally: 'Let all your behaviour be such as even pagans can recognize as good, and then, whereas they malign you as criminals now, they will come to see for themselves that you live good lives, and will give glory to God in the day when he comes to hold assize . . . It is the will of God that by your good conduct you should put ignorance and stupidity to silence.'

You want every fellow toiler to give glory to God. You have a sense of mission more compulsive than that of the most dedicated

atheist agitator, because you believe that Christ is the Saviour of
all.

·   ·   ·   ·

The Russian Baptist thinks in Biblical terms. A convert is a man
or woman who has been 'born again', undergone a personal experience of repentance and faith. You confess the Lord Jesus with
your mouth and believe in your heart that God raised him from
the dead and prove your faith by your manner of life before the
Church will admit to baptism and thus to full membership. The
claim that the Russian Baptist is the fastest growing in the world
must be viewed in this context, that membership is never passive
or incidental.

Most, but by no means all, converts spring from families with
at least some religious belief, young men and women who have
passed the gamut of atheist schooling[1] yet accept Christ as Saviour
—by deliberate, courageous decision. In the Soviet Union religious upbringing is not enough; lukewarm loyalty or passive
discipleship, which in the West may hold younger members of a
family to the fringes of the congregation, quickly dissolves into
passive atheism.

That there is widespread spiritual desire in a nation where
Christian churches are thinly scattered is evident from some of the
letters written to broadcasters of the F.E.B.C.

'Today,' runs a letter received in Tokyo from an industrial
worker in Siberia, 'I with reverence for the first time in my mortal
life through all the noise of the ether clearly heard the whole cycle
of your short programme, dictated by the spiritual wisdom of
God. The appealing sermons I could understand rather clearly,
but I am sorry to say that the singing was submerged by atmo-
spheric noises [jamming?] and many words were lost to me.' The
writer was a Russian in his late thirties, married with children. He
went on: 'I feel lonely in my spiritual searching and would be
happy to correspond with you . . . I am praying for the Lord's
grace that this letter might reach your address, because the one
and only reason of my writing to you is my most fervent searching
for Spiritual Wisdom, searching for the inexhaustible source of

[1] See Chapters XV and XVI.

Immortality, containing the essence of all Existing, and in which dwells the Lord Himself, whose are the glory and might . . .' After the signature the writer added the age-old Russian greeting: 'Christ's peace be with you!'

An actor then playing in a place on the Turk-Sib Railway wrote: 'I would love to have books from which I can obtain knowledge. Who wouldn't like to know more? I am interested in all people's religions, but up to now I can't comprehend why every creed or confession of faith is different. I have long desired to read the Bible—to know and learn its meaning, but have never seen or had a Bible. I borrowed a Bible Commentary and read same.'

A technologist in Kazakhstan 'heard on the radio your radio programme and felt my soul disturbed. I also would like to serve our Lord, but I have no Bible, no literature and I am asking you to send me a Bible and religious literature.'

The quaintest letter came from a person evidently without slightest contact with any Church: 'Dear radio-preaching station "Voice of the East" (I am writing to you) with great permission! The one that is writing this is an earth inhabitant in the Soviet Union. Please be so kind as to inform me in detail of the purpose of your speaking-preaching station and her history. Did Christ give you permission for existence of your esteemed station at any time? Also be so kind to send me any sort of literature of the esteemed-respected god Christ.'

.   .   .   .

Since propagation of religion is unlawful, the Baptist pursues his mission by friendship. Transparent integrity and beauty of character may attract, but, by themselves, not normally convert, though they may lead to a workmate asking the exact sources of a man's joy and endurance, asking why he does not swear or drink, why he lacks resentment or anger if teased. The Baptist will answer, but must guard against open, illegal, persuasion; he hopes instead to invite his friend to the prayer-house, as he has every legal right.

Friendship and concern for neighbours are the Baptists' great weapons. Even atheists admit their persistence. 'The worshippers of Christ,' grumbled *Red Star*, the Army newspaper, 'want to get their greedy claws on everybody around them. They are prepared to work for years to get hold of the person they want.' *Molodoi Kommunist* (*Young Communist*) complained that sectarians go fishing in the streets, in the trams, in the trains. 'They talk to people in flattering tones. They send their representatives to find out which people in the hospital have no visitors, and then go to see them full of sympathy and understanding.'

A Young Communist called Alexei Sibirko, an efficient driver for the Autotrust of Dzhambul in Central Asia, a good athlete, full of energy, went one night to the town club. A man there got drunk and began to mishandle two girls. Alexei hurried to their defence and when walking back through darkened streets to his home was leaped on by the infuriated drunkard and stabbed in the back. Militiamen found him; but his spine had been damaged and he left hospital a hopeless cripple. The head of the Autotrust pensioned him off, scrawled 'Dismissed' on his card, forgot him. No former workmate came near.

Dzhambul has a strong Baptist church, reported more than 900 strong by *Kazakhstanskaya Pravda* of June 2nd 1963. They have a choir of 100, almost half of whom are young people, they are active in the building college, a sewing school, in many collectives, including the city food combine, the leather combine—and No. 8 automobile base.

Autotrust Baptists heard about Alexei Sibirko and told the pastor, who after calling on the now bedridden athlete, invited two churchwomen to devote their spare time to nursing him. Alexei was grateful. They became friends, and when the sisters talked of the source of their friendship he listened eagerly. He was unable to get to church, but the pastor told the congregation about him, and they were raising funds to send him to a spinal specialist in Moscow when the Autotrust Komsomol learned he had fallen under the influence of sectarians. Komsomol intervened. Alexei was persuaded to tell his Baptist nurses to stop visiting.

A woman in the Crimea neared despair because her husband was an incorrigible drunkard. One of her neighbours, a Baptist, invited her to the church. To be among friends who abhorred liquor was a deep relief. Before long she testified to faith; a sober husband sat on the men's side in church. Her conversion was lasting. But, in the gleeful words of that journal with a mouthful of a name: *V Pomoshch Politicheskomu Samoobrazovaniyu* (*Aid to Political Self-Education*) 'the Baptists' God proved to be helpless against Bacchus and the "brother" soon appeared again in a "happy" state'.

A Baptist woman was having a baby. In a Russian maternity hospital no visitor, not even the husband, is admitted for fear of infection throughout the compulsory fourteen days of lying-in. Husbands, parents and friends send flowers and fruit. The Baptist noticed another woman who had no flowers or fruit, no message of love or congratulation, no word from her husband. The Baptist shared the good things lavished on her by family and church members (Russian Baptists are some of the most generous people in the world) and then sent out a message. Next day a bunch of flowers and a basket of fruit arrived for the lonely woman. The Baptist learned that her husband was not even going to fetch his wife and baby. They took them home by car. To the church it was a natural gesture backed by prayer and leading to the mother's happy baptism.

In a city of Central Asia a man was murdered. The young widow married again and moved to a small house which was thinly partitioned from the next. Through the wall she heard singing. She used to look forward to the nights when they sang, and at length asked her neighbours what it was all about. They said, 'Wouldn't you like to join us when we sing?' She sang and became friends. They invited her to church. In due course she, her second husband and all her children were converted; man and wife both now serve on the church council.

Alexei the crippled ex-driver of Dzhambul had never been to church. The drunkard's wife, the young mother and the murdered man's remarried widow, all of whom became firm Christians, had attended church frequently before they passed (in typical Bible phrases which would come to a Russian Baptist's mind) 'from darkness to light, and from the power of Satan unto God'. The fact of prior church attendance is not incidental: evangelism in Russia is the work of a congregation rather than of an individual. Conversions occur silently during the preaching or during the hymns or the prayers. 'Scarcely a sermon goes by,' I have heard claimed, 'without someone coming to the Lord.'

Conversions are not circumscribed by the church buildings.

One man now a pastor was shovelling manure by himself in Siberia when it struck him that this was what the Prodigal Son must have done; and then that he had never followed the Prodigal Son's example, going to his Father and saying, 'Father, I have sinned . . .' He knelt, prayed the Prodigal Son's prayer and knew the Father had received him. This future pastor, on rising from his knees, was worried because there was no one in sight to whom he could instantly confess his faith!

Nor are conversions curbed by absence of a presbyter to preach.

A Baptist family moves to a village where no church is open. They sing and pray in their home. Neighbours join, others gather outside in summer to enjoy the singing. On reaching twenty members (who must be over eighteen years old) the new church seeks registration with the Council for Religious Cults, its being technically unlawful once it has passed beyond a private gathering of friends. To qualify for registration the church must occupy separate premises for 'the performance of the cult'. Two next-door neighbours may offer slices of their gardens for building if the local soviet (representing the State as landowner) agrees. Even if a building is put up, registration may be refused, often because the regional soviet wishes to retain power to extinguish the new church swiftly.

Without registration no official pastor may be appointed. An unregistered Church functions and thrives, the responsibility of the laity with occasional visits from the pastor of the nearest city or the Senior Presbyter, who may have nearly twice as many unregistered groups as official churches. Meanwhile one of the members has moved to a new job, a new village—and the process is repeated. If the Russian Baptist Church had no other message for Churches of the West it could be this: that an instructed, spiritually virile laity can mean an expanding church even in a unsympathetic environment.

108

A Soviet Communist or a Western rationalist who strays into a Russian Baptist church may say what he will. A convinced Christian, whatever his disagreement on points of doctrine or practice, his denominational label, will recognize the unmistakable signs of the Spirit of God: 'Surely the Lord is in this place . . . this is none other than the house of God, and this is the gate of heaven.' The Communist may snarl or sneer about mass persuasion, telepathy or a trick, the Baptists believe in what they call the sovereign grace of God; they read in the Bible of the exceeding greatness of His power; they expect Him to transform men and women and, whatever detractors claim, men and women are transformed.

It is all so uncontrived. As a postscript here is first-hand evidence which owes nothing to the impressions of a foreign visitor—a letter written by an office girl in her mid-twenties after hearing a short-wave broadcast: 'I was touched very much by the story of the very sick little girl and about the fact that spiritual babies have to strive for survival and strengthening in faith all the time. As for me, your talk has been very useful and that's because I am a spiritual baby too. It is only two years since I found the truth. The Lord sent a girl friend to me who brought me to the Baptist church. Here in the Baptist church at —— I'm humbly serving the Lord.'

CHAPTER XIII

HAMMER AND CROSS

A FACTORY hand in the capital of the Estonian S.S.R., Tallinn
(formerly Reval), was a Baptist and a great reader, having had
the advantage of upbringing in the days of Estonia's independence
when books circulated freely. He did not hide his scorn of the
atheist intellectual position. His fellow toilers thereupon arranged
in the later months of 1960 a debate unusual in a Communist
state: the leading atheists allowed the Baptist to put his case beside
theirs, which was propounded by a strong team, including an
astronomer, a physician and a philosopher.

The factory hands, with their spice of pre-1940 individualism,
awarded applause where it was due, Party line or not. And the
Baptist won the debate. To every argument of the atheists he had
an answer which his mates cheered to the echo. The astronomer
with his 'no God to be seen in space', the physician with gibes at
prayer, the philosopher whose long-winded materialism sounded
dreariest of all were routed.

A stenographer recorded the discussion, but not a word
appeared in the Press. Someone sent the stenographer's report to
the flourishing Baptist church of Kuibyshev (the former wartime
capital on the Volga), where it was circulated in the factories as a
twenty-six-page pamphlet.

This incident highlights the heartening truth that Russian
Baptists are on the offensive.

Theirs may be a rough-hewn outlook. But they have a fervour
often lacking in the West and do not let convictions sleep. They
have their victories which the Soviet Press will not, and the sole
Baptist publication may not, record. The Press blazes their defeats.
The conflict continues daily in industry, in the professions and,
especially, in the sphere of education and youth.

By Communist theory 'religious survivals' are expected in agricultural, rare in industrial districts. The Baptists grow faster in industrial cities—an unpalatable fact admitted officially by inference only, as when *Literaturnaya Gazeta* criticized the atheists' society because in the famous steel city of Magnitogorsk in the Urals, 'the hundreds of atheist lectures attended by thousands of people cannot compete with the influence of the local Baptists', or when in November 1963 at Klaipeda, the former East Prussian Memel, a Communist Party conference heard a delegate emphasize 'the great damage that was being inflicted by religious sectarians, who had succeeded in catching in their nets certain unstable people from the milk combine, the "Trinchyai" factory and the canning factory'.

To be a Christian in industry is to risk your job. At Rovno in the north-western Ukraine two Baptist girls worked in the same shop at a large dressmaking factory. They were energetic skilled machinists, and, moreover, where once had been two Baptists, now there were four. The output in the shop rose above the 'norm' and headed towards winning for the factory the coveted title of Communist Labour Collective when, in the latter part of 1962, the chairman of the factory committee happened to receive an order to reduce staff. Comrade Sidorenko cast around and decided that girls not ideologically correct might lengthen the odds for the title. The Baptists were fired. Another woman, Comrade Shilo, was a leading production hand, a delegate on the insurance committee, a trade unionist, regular at lectures and meetings, full of good works by Communist standards. Her name appeared on the list for High Production awards, and Chairman Sidorenko crossed it off—because for a time she had frequented the Baptist church.

This particular chairman was scolded by *Science and Religion* in 1962, yet the same atheist magazine in September 1963 remarks approvingly that the rank and file believer 'can be worked on at a meeting and threatened with dismissal from his job . . . The religious professionals are another thing; they cannot be summoned to trade union meetings. They cannot be threatened with dismissal.' Bluster and the boot, it seems, are correct if they lead to recantation. They seldom do.

N. Y. Shevchenko was a driving instructor at the car instruction centre of Melitopol, Ukraine, a good worker of seven years standing with no blemish of accident or inefficiency on his sheet. He attended the prayer-house, but was not a strong believer; an atheist comrade believed him ripe for recovery. A new director took over the car centre in the summer of 1963, and within a few days issued Shevchenko an ultimatum. 'Either you renounce Baptistism or there is no place for you in my centre.' Shevchenko took no notice. Shortly afterwards a foreman reported him for a mistake in driving. A few days later he was reported by another worker. Then he was told a complaint had been lodged against him by a pupil. Director Poliektov, looking out of his window as Shevchenko drove in, sent out a message criticizing some error or another; the poor man's clean sheet rapidly filled with reprimands.

Poliektov summoned Shevchenko to the office. 'In the District Party Committee,' barked Poliektov, 'they are calling me the director of the Baptist centre because of you! So let us decide—Will you renounce your religion?'

Shevchenko's hesitations vanished. He had sought where lay truth, with the Communists or the Christians. The injustice of faked reprimands, the pressure of a director who wished to crush conscience, tore the bandage from his eyes.

'No,' he said, 'I will not.'

'Very well. Send me your resignation.'

Shevchenko, out of work, went forward for baptism.

Discrimination is not general, but may occur wherever a man in authority tires of slow, ineffective educational methods of converting believers. A series of such incidents occurred in late 1962 or early 1963 among the blast furnaces and grim array of belching chimneys at Dneprodzerzhinsk, which, though next city up the Dnieper from Dnepropetrovsk, where Gaevskaya organized her energetic agitation[1] and without a single Orthodox church still open, could only secure two or three people for atheist seminars despite a letter to all local organizations. As for the Atheists' Advice Centre, 'Has anyone come? No, no one has come! We advertised over the radio and in the newspaper. A duty roster is posted up in the room and what happens? An agitator, a member

[1] See Chapter III.

of the Atheists' Club, comes in, sits down for an hour or two, no one comes, he puts on his hat and good-bye . . .'

In the Dneprodzerzhinsk State District Power Station a skilled toiler called I. K. Petlya, who was a Baptist, had a reputation for efficiency and energy. Atheists attempted to secure his dismissal. An electrical engineer whose technical qualifications, high standards and devotion to duty entitled him to a rise from seventy roubles a month to eighty met a novel form of wage restraint. The Power Station office told him: 'Leave the sect and you will get more pay.' At the end of the next month the wage office sent for him: 'Are you ready for more pay? Cut away from the Baptists and you will get another ten roubles.' He could have complained to higher authority, but he knew better. And ten roubles, he chuckled, was not worth as much as thirty pieces of silver.

In the nearby coke and chemical works an atheist tried another trick. He went early to the canteen and surreptitiously filled a sectarian's tumbler with vodka, which, of course, looks like water. The atheist rubbed his hands with glee; the usual small vodka glass would make a Baptist's head swim, a tumbler would have him singing and staggering; a drunken Baptist would discredit the faith and surely be dismissed from his sect, to fall gratefully into the arms of the atheists.

The Baptist took a sip and pushed the glass away. How the atheist thought the powerful taste of vodka could be disguised remains a mystery!

The Power Station took the palm in Dneprodzerzhinsk for ham-handed action. A toiler called A. A. Karas, who probably was in his twenties, surrendered to constant nagging by the head of his shift, stopped going to the prayer-house and at a political education meeting admitted, with some prodding from the foreman, that he was renouncing the Baptist faith.

The atheists hailed him a brand plucked from the burning, as it were. The Ukrainian *Agitator's Notebook* and a brochure, *The New is Conquering*, featured his rescue from religious obscurantism, the local paper reported the good news, it was taken up with gusto by the regional newspaper, *Dneprovskaya Pravda*. Possibly good old Gaevskaya herself wrote the story. And the

Baptist pastor in Dneprodzerzhinsk read in the paper of his friend Karas bringing atheistic booklets and Marxist-Leninist classics to the well-equipped new apartment he had just been allocated. The description of Karas' house-warming for the lads of his shift was mouth-watering.

The pastor went round to the backstreet where he had often called in the past, climbed the stairs of the crowded tenement where Karas had lived with his wife and children in a typically poky room with kitchenette, and knocked on the door. Karas opened it.

Next day the pastor took two or three leading Baptists to the chairman of the Power Station. Very politely, very firmly, they said that Karas must really be given a new apartment, or an apology should be published in the Press.

The town rocked with the scandal—a revealing indication of the average Russian's contempt for the militant atheist minority. The last laugh was with the Baptists—Karas, still living in his old apartment, rejoined them and let his mates know it.

Moscow's comment was scathing. Dneprodzerzhinsk had claimed fifty apostates in five years, yet the Baptists had recruited thirty new members in twelve months of 1962–63: 'It emerges that the sectarians are working better than the atheists.'

. . . .

An atheist wrote an account in the 'fifties in *Literaturnaya Gazeta*, 'The Preacher from Kolodnya', which unconsciously shows the boredom felt by ordinary industrial managers when anti-religious agitators attempt to discredit a good worker because he is an active Christian.

The atheist attended a service in the cramped little prayer-house of a village near Smolensk. His description, when disinfected of the inevitable Party line ('furtive movements' . . . 'malevolent grin' . . . 'her whole face shone with craft and cunning' . . . 'their voices sounded dull and depressed') provides an authentic vignette of a meeting in winter: the close-packed rows, the narrow aisles leading to a reading desk covered by a yellow cloth, the texts on the walls, grannies in head-scarves, an old man with straggly beard, the mixed choir of young men and women singing to the lead of 'a short girl in a red dress'; the thick, heavy air and the two hours' long service.

'One song followed another. One's head swam from the heat. Suddenly, along with a draught of cold air, a small movement went through the assembly. I glanced at the door. On the threshold there stood a young man in a sports jacket with a zip fastener, from one of whose pockets there glittered the metal top of a fountain pen. With an accustomed movement he combed a shock of light hair, blew through his comb,[1] and tucked it away in the hip pocket of his trousers, stuffed into high boots. Outwardly he was no different from thousands of young people whom you can meet in factories, in institutions or in students' lecture rooms . . .'

The young man mounted the reading desk. He raised his eyes heavenwards and said quietly: 'My dear brothers and sisters! May blessings be multiplied to you . . .' The atheist agitator, who was particularly shocked when the preacher 'even appealed to the people to pray for their enemies', totally missed the point of the sermon and at the close of the service turned to his neighbour to ask if the young man had ever gone to a Soviet school.

'And to the technical college!' the neighbour answered. 'Our Andryusha is a building technician.' The agitator could hardly believe it.

Next day he called on the secretary of the Party organization at the city building trust, who obligingly sent for the file on Andrei Semkin, senior engineer of the capital construction section.

'Well!' said the secretary, 'He seems a good lad. Aged twenty-six—the youngest specialist in our collective. Active, a good mixer, politically educated. Biography good. Peasant stock. Completed the Civil Building Technical College and came to us a year later. You know that we don't allow the cadres to vegetate. We develop them. He was promoted not long ago . . . He seems all right on the social side. Attends the course of study of fundamentals, speaks

[1] This little touch to the story is rather clever if the journalist wants to discredit the young man: in Russia combing your hair in public is uncultured. I saw a militiaman at the Kursky terminus in Moscow rebuke a fellow for doing it. 'Put that comb away, citizen,' he said sharply. The man looked hurt, but obeyed.

on political subjects to the collective, carries out the work given him.'

'He attends the course?'

'Not for the first year, either! You should see the papers he writes. We hold him up as an example. Thorough!' The secretary called in two Party colleagues, who enthusiastically supported his report on Semkin: his papers were as correct and clean as himself. It was true he had not joined the Komsomol; there was a rumour he was a sectarian, they had not pressed.

When, however, the agitator indignantly taxed them with the possibility that Semkin indeed was a sectarian they smiled tolerantly. 'No, what are you thinking about! If there was such a tendency the school, the technical college, the whole of our daily life would undoubtedly have re-educated him. If only you could meet him, but he is away just now. Just look at his photo.'

They probably knew perfectly well he was a sectarian. To the agitator Semkin was a hypocritical 'double dealer and witch doctor'; to his bosses in the builders' collective he was one of the best technicians, of outstanding character and an enthusiastic student of his country's social and political system. If a believer, that was his own affair.

.   .   .   .

Academic or professional qualifications are comparatively few among sectarians, who are found mostly in the ranks of plain toilers. The very fact of being an active believer may bar higher education.[1] The Kuibyshev Baptists, however, have no less than forty-five members with higher education, according to *Science and Religion*, including several doctors and engineers and a former teacher of Russian language and literature.

A thirty-three-year-old engineer at a Kuibyshev factory manufacturing spare parts for tractors was made to stand out at a works meeting where colleagues accused him of 'religious propaganda' and Party officials gave him a stiff dressing down. A young and capable woman engineer and designer called Vera, a quiet girl who did not proselytize, was hauled before the head of the design office, Comrade Denisov, on discovery that she was a

[1] See Chapter XVI.

Baptist. At a general meeting 'the girl's religious views became the subject of public research by everyone with a mind to it. They began to fire questions at her and frequently with a complete lack of courtesy:

' "When did you become a believer?"

' "How could the Virgin Mary become pregnant without ceasing to be a maiden?"

' "How can you believe in man's origin from God when you know that man originated from monkeys?"

' "Aren't you ashamed to take examinations on social subjects?"

' "This is how you have repaid your institute!" '

She was threatened with transfer to the heavy work of the casting shop. When an anti-religious agitator visited the works he would be sent straight from his lecture to the design shop, and Vera placed in front of him for a harangue.

One of the doctors at Kuibyshev, N. F. Shmurov, has a strong dash of moral courage, for he has openly stated: 'The deeper I probe into natural science, the more I am convinced that the Baptist view is correct.' He also talks on spiritual matters with patients at his clinic, just as would a Christian doctor in England or America. When *Science and Religion* sent a reporter to interview him, Dr. Shmurov declined to be drawn into controversy. The reporter goaded and taunted him. The doctor did not lose his temper.

Nor did the young Baptist theatre sister at Klintsy, the textile centre in Bryansk region, Central Russia, who clearly impressed, in spite of himself, a Moscow agitator present when she was interviewed by the deputy head of the local Party's Ideological Department, the gross and overbearing Comrade Zhitlov. The interview opened and continued with abusive monologues from Zhitlov on the usual lines: 'How can you believe in God if our cosmonauts have been flying in the cosmos and have found no God there?' etc., etc. 'During all these monologues,' writes the Moscow man in *Science and Religion* for December 1963, 'Lyuda preserved a guarded silence.' Zhitlov at length asked one question, which the Moscow agitator thought fatuous, and then said, 'Throw up your faith and you will begin to experience real life.'

'Lyuda, evidently desiring,' writes the Muscovite, 'to know

what the man she is talking with understands by a "real" life, informs him that she is trying to improve her work and that she reads the latest medical literature.

' "We will check on this. We will check with your ticket in the library," ' came the answer.

Zhitlov then interviewed her friend at work, a Komsomol, who confirmed that Lyuda certainly read a lot; she bought her books too. The Muscovite chuckled—the check-up in the library would be useless. The head doctor, a woman, was yet more enthusiastic: 'Yes, Lyuda regularly reads the latest medical literature, at times even before I do. She is a capable, conscientious and honest worker and selflessly loves children. We were convinced of this when Lyuda worked in the kindergarten.'

Comrade Zhitlov's coarse-grained methods reflect the normal Party attitude to Christians who are proficient in a scientific discipline. As the Muscovite commented, Zhitlov did not show heart-felt concern for her rescue from religion 'but annoyance that in a reputable medical establishment a responsible position should be held by a Baptist girl and that it was now necessary to spend time on her'.

Zhitlov at least did not follow the practice of the head doctor of a hospital near Kursk, the railway centre in the Black Earth country, who 'challenged, demanded and warned', and finally called in the chairman of the local soviet, accompanied by a militiaman, yet failed to force the recantation of his epidemiologist, 'an educated and cultured man [who] believes in God'.

Epidemiologist and theatre sister did not yield to pressure. And were most unlikely to yield to persuasion if a broadcast on Moscow Radio in August 1963 is typical of atheist attempts to prove that religion is a danger to health. The level of argument may be gauged by its opening passage, in which the speaker traced Christianity's hostility to medicine throughout history, stating that it had prohibited dissection (true of Pope Boniface in 1297, but hardly relevant to modern medicine), had condemned anaesthesia (although in historic fact chloroform was discovered by a staunch evangelical Christian, Sir James Simpson) and had enforced a ban on vaccination in Britain until the present century, a ridiculous statement, since vaccination, discovered by Jenner, who publicly thanked God for using him, was compulsory in Britain from 1853 until 1948.

Despite the danger (were the broadcast right) to the health of hundreds of thousands of people, there are Christian doctors and scientists in Russia, writers and artists, too. There cannot be politicians, for a politician must be an atheist and Party member. The numbers of Christians in the intelligentsia is growing. When Russian Baptists were told that in Britain of the 'sixties the Gospel tended to spread from intellectuals to workers the Russians replied: 'It is exactly the other way round with us. It is going up from working people to the intelligentsia. Just a little.'

CHAPTER XIV

RED ARMY CHRISTIANS?

EARLY in 1963 a young man called Vladimir Umantsev was conscripted into the Red Army. A war orphan, he had been brought up by childless foster-parents and then went out on his own. Later he discovered his mother, who had lost him as a baby during the German invasion. A lonely childhood had been made bearable because his foster-parents were believers; he had a gift for verse and spent time writing hymns and religious poems.

The other recruits of the draft discovered Vladimir's poems and teased him, his lot thus far differing little from that of any similar youth in the barrack room of a Western army. The company commander, however, heard of his faith and at once consulted a brother-officer, the battalion expert, who sent for Vladimir and firmly but quite gently pointed out the gravity of his position—a believer in an atheist army—and gave him atheist literature. He had Vladimir transferred to his company.

A long period of indoctrination began. At political education lectures the officers brought Vladimir forward to trip up his reasoning, which proved shallow; faith had been primarily a feeling. The sergeants gave him a hard time, for until he should abandon Christianity his patriotism and reliability were suspect. Little by little Vladimir's convictions were eroded.

Radio Volga (for Soviet Forces in Germany) brought him to the microphone on September 9th 1963 to tell how he had 'now found the right way to life and the right approach to people'.

The Soviet Armed Forces are about the most thoroughly indoctrinated of any sector in the nation. 'Scientific-atheistic' knowledge being one of the subjects of compulsory political education, a soldier, sailor or airman serves in an atmosphere conditioning him to reject belief: 'every young man on completing his service in the Armed Forces should return home a convinced atheist'. The Services do not hesitate to emphasize that religion and patriotism are incompatible. Even after the signing of the 1963 Test Ban Treaty the Ministry of Defence issued a virulent pamphlet asserting that the leaders of many sects were connected with American imperialism and engaged in espionage and ideological subversion against the U.S.S.R. It described Jehovah's Witnesses and spent much space unmasking the words and deeds of the Evangelical Christians/Baptists, whom, it implied, were financed from Washington, where world Baptist leaders justify the aggressive foreign policy of the United States and come out against the fighters for peace and against progress for mankind. 'Many Baptists are used as American spies.'

Every able-bodied Soviet citizen is conscripted for active service lasting between two and five years, depending on the arm of the Forces to which he is drafted, and thus, except for the trifling minority who refuse and take the consequences, all young Christians, if fit, enter this pressure chamber of the conscience. The story of V. Yu. Tikhomirov, which he told in 1962, shows what can happen.

Tikhomirov entered the Red Army as bravely determined as Peter at the Last Supper: 'Though all men shall be offended because of Thee yet will I never be offended . . . Though I should die for Thee yet will I not deny Thee.' When his comrades in the platoon chafed him he bore it cheerfully, glad to suffer shame for Christ's name.

One evening a film was on. He stayed alone in the barrack room to pray and read his hymn-book (he was one of the many thousands of Christians unable to acquire a Bible or Testament). The sergeant found him.

'Why are you not with the others at the Club? Are you ill?'

'I am very well, I thank God,' replied Tikhomirov piously. 'But worldly amusements do not attract me.'

The sergeant concluded that the boy was deliberately pretending to be dull in order to be transferred to the reserve-troops: a malingerer. 'You come along with me,' he said.

Tikhomirov guessed he would be taken before the Zampolit (Political Administration Branch), and prepared for the worst. He picked up soap, towel, toothbrush, hymn-book and put them in his greatcoat.

The sergeant looked puzzled. 'Where are you going with all that, lad?'

'Where it pleases God to send me. Take me!'

The sergeant marched him to the Zampolit office and reported the facts, from prayers to toothbrush. The Captain in charge asked Tikhomirov mildly, 'Where do you want to go with your things?'

'I'm a Christian and shall always be a Christian! Do what you like with me. Take me to the main-guard!'

The war-scarred Captain said nothing. He looked at him, his big dark eyes expressive of understanding and concern. And smiled, a charming, spontaneous smile. 'Sergeant, you may fall out now . . . Tikhomirov, come and sit over here on the sofa . . . Feeling homesick?'

'Yes.'

'I used to be homesick too. I used to write home several times a day. I wonder now that I did it! What was your job? . . . In the forest? Why, that's what I did.'

The Comrade-Captain chatted away about the forest, and about working with cattle, not a word about religion. Tikhomirov liked him, felt he must be a Christian at heart.

When the boy was dismissed he praised God for a new friend. They had many subsequent conversations. The Captain knew that Tikhomirov prayed after each, that he went to the Baptist prayer-house in the town. It made no difference. They went fishing together, into the town together. Only when the friendship had developed did the Captain, as if casually, touch on religion. The boy's admiration led to questions. The Captain would answer briefly and simply with all the gentle force that a strong older man who has sifted his ideas may exert over a hero-worshipping youth whose convictions have been earnest but second-hand and whose education has been limited: he had left school at thirteen; it is not always easy for a believer to be admitted to the higher grades. Tikhomirov was most impressed when the Captain showed him what the *Large Soviet Encyclopaedia* had to say about the mythical Christ.

Tikhomirov, his military service over, is now an atheist propagandist in Odessa. He has not yet heard the cock crow thrice.

The Captain who 'converted' him was an exception. A more usual road to apostasy is by pressure of barrack-room intolerance backed by normal indoctrination lectures. Yet the number of ex-conscripts who remain or become active church members on return to civil life proves indoctrination to be less than wholly successful, nor is a Red Army or Navy uniform rare in the churches and prayer-houses of Moscow and Leningrad. The pressure is not always exerted strongly. Individual units of the Armed Forces are often as impatient with atheism, or as indifferent, as individual collectives in industry and agriculture. Germans under Russian occupation in the frightful aftermath of the Second World War knew at least one Red Army officers' mess where Christian services and Bible studies took place openly every day. When Marshal Zhukov was Minister of Defence (1955–57) little attention was paid to atheist propaganda, but at the close of 1958 the Main Political Administration of the Army and Navy held a conference to co-ordinate and strengthen appropriate agitation.

Servicemen have become believers while serving, but firm evidence is scanty. No chaplains exist, naturally. I recall an unguarded moment late at night when I asked a group of Russian Christians about religion in the Forces and chatted about the British Chaplain-General's department and parade services being no longer compulsory and—the atmosphere had frozen. 'Oh,' said someone slowly when I stopped talking. 'You don't ask questions about *religion* in the *Army*!'

.   .   .   .

Officers of the Red Army or Navy are generally members of the Communist Party or Young Communists, and thus committed to be merciless opponents of 'religious survivals'.

A true story was printed in *Red Star* which, if looked at from the angle opposite to that of its writer, discloses the approximate facts of an officer's conversion and subsequent dilemma.

Aleksandr Lada was rated on his service record 'one of the best officers' of a commissariat unit. He had been a Party member since the age of twenty-two. Year by year his sheet showed him 'ideologically sound', 'politically educated', that he actively shared in the socialist discussions of his unit and worked to improve his 'military political knowledge'. He had married a charming wife and they were raising a large family. Lada's brother officers knew his wife was a believer, thought of her none the less highly, and when the colonel wanted a talk given to the soldiers' wives on the right upbringing of children he turned to her as an obvious choice. Lada received appointment as unit Party secretary, being closely interested in the political education of the troops.

He had attended a Baptist church occasionally with his wife and did not object when she preferred that the children should not join the Pioneers. When they moved to a garrison town near Vladivostok Lada grew progressively more interested in the faith that made his home gloriously happy and his wife so good a mother despite difficulties of a soldiering existence. In 1955 he gave the loyalty of his heart and will to Christ and joined the Evangelical Christians/Baptists, and in 1957, having passed the probationary two years, he was ready for baptism. He took local leave to Vladivostok, changed into civilian clothes. Soon after sunrise on a misty winter morning he went down to a quiet beach of Golden Horn Bay, where a group of Baptists had gathered round their pastor and the candidates for baptism; Baptists in Vladivostok were under very considerable pressure in 1957, and the prayer-house of this particular congregation may have been taken away, thus explaining why they used the sea for baptistry.

On that cold morning, in a winter sea, Major A. S. Lada was baptized at the age of thirty-eight.

He did not resign from the Communist Party. No one does. To offer resignation, as no longer an atheist, would have caused an uproar in District Command followed by certain expulsion and, because of the scandal inflicted on the Army, the probable ruin of his career. Nor did Lada personally view the matter as a dilemma of conscience. He was still an ardent Communist in that he, like very many of his fellow citizens who knew no other social system except through the distorting mirror of the Soviet Press and text-books, believed Marxism-Leninism to be the finest economic order possible to man. He regarded Communism's anti-religious element as an error explicable by the circumstances of Russian history in Tsarist times, an error which must one day be eliminated. For

Lada, pure Communism and pure Christianity should converge; the ranting of militant atheists saddened him.

He continued Party secretary. He had the sense not to preach Christianity in his political lectures to the troops: he merely omitted the anti-religious sections of the syllabus. Colonel and brother officers did not mind. They knew Lada no longer frequented the Club, spent his leisure at home in the happy family circle: 'they lived quietly in an old-fashioned way and they had their own cow'. Every evening ended with a bright little service of song and prayers.

District Command's Zampolit discovered that Lada's lectures lacked atheism. The whole matter emerged under investigation. Lada was expelled from the Party 'for taking part in religious ceremonies, for concealing his membership of a sect and for playing a double game'.

Expulsion made no difference in the unit. They did not even inscribe it on his record sheet!

His period of military service was completed shortly, he received honourable discharge to the reserve, retired with his family to the little town of Saki in the Crimea and took a job at the chemical works. The local Evangelical Christian/Baptists received him warmly, and when he could not find a house roomy enough for his large family and was leased a plot of land by intervention of military headquarters the congregation helped him build. He became their staunch supporter and had a nice little habit of going to church openly in reservist uniform, an unashamed 'soldier of the Lord'—at which the town atheists set up a howl, which is how *Red Star* heard.

By any standard except that of the militant atheists and their lackeys in the Press, Major A. S. Lada is an honourable, devotedly loyal ex-serviceman, a good husband and father, a first-rate citizen of the U.S.S.R.[1]

[1] At Leningrad in 1954 two young soldiers told Dr. Ernest Payne that there were many believers in the Red Army, and asked him to carry greetings to Christians in the British Army.

CHAPTER XV

'SUFFER LITTLE CHILDREN . . .'

THE parents of the children at the secondary school of a small town called Gotsk near Minsk in Belorussia met to elect a new member to the parents' committee. They needed someone whose home was happy and well ordered, who understood children, appreciated good teaching and could contribute to discussion of matters to be brought before the headmaster or on which the school authorities consulted parents. The head teacher of a department, Comrade Skorobogatov (he happened also to be the leader of the school's atheistic section), rose to suggest a suitable person: he named the presbyter of the local Baptist church. The presbyter was elected. This same school circulated to the senior students a questionnaire which included: 'What do you want to be?' Two replied, 'A preacher.'

Such incidents might seem normal and unexceptionable in schools of the West, where a local clergyman will be an obvious choice for the parents' committee, and embryo preachers, if their characters honour their ambition, are encouraged.

Poor Comrade Skorobogatov of Gotsk was pilloried before the Russian nation.

At a plenum of the Komsomol Central Committee in July 1963 he was held up to obloquy by no less than S. P. Pavlov, First Secretary of the All-Union Komsomol, as a specimen-product of the widespread complacent assumption 'that religion will die of itself'. 'One cannot console oneself, Comrades,' said Pavlov, 'with the fact that the basic contingent of believers are elderly people . . . Recently the servants of the religious cult have intensified their religious indoctrination of children, using believing parents for this purpose.' His words were echoed on October 10th 1963 by another exalted figure of the educational world, Mikhail Petrovich Kashin, Deputy Minister of Education in the Russian Federal Republic: 'Religious influence,' he said in a broadcast, 'is a terrible enemy which we often underestimate. Do not think, Comrades, that the Church and the sects influence only the older generation.' He cited facts and issued a stirring call that 'the schools—and all of us—must wage a persistent struggle against [religion], and must not be inactive in the hope that the Church will die away by itself'.

The incident at Gotsk and the words of the two educational dignitaries spotlight the core of the conflict in the Soviet Union of the 'sixties. Atheist State and vigorous Christianity are battling for the souls of children and youth. The State is alarmed. Pressure increases.

From the earliest days of a child's life the State would like to exert atheist influence. Because christening in church is still frequent (among Orthodox: Baptists, of course, do not practise infant baptism), and in Party eyes is 'a degrading, barbaric and pernicious ceremony', Leningrad Soviet decided in August 1963 to open two 'Palaces of the Newly Born', complete with a 'beautiful and solemn ritual' during which the birth certificate would be presented to the parents, together with the congratulations of the City soviet and a medal portraying Lenin in an armoured car with the Neva river for background. By mid-1964 no special 'Baby Palace' had yet been built, but similar presentations were already held in Latvia as part of the nation-wide campaign, begun in 1959, to offset religious ceremonies by colourful secular substitutes, while Lvov (formerly a city of Poland) claims great success for its marriage and family 'Palace of Happiness'. On the other hand, in Kazakhstan, though a third of the population is Moslem, one-tenth of all babies born in the first five months of 1963 were christened and in Tula, the famous ironware town about 120 miles south of Moscow, the proportion was as high as one-third, according to a newspaper of June 5th.

Christening can often be dismissed as the initiative of grannies. As a Western correspondent in Moscow said, 'In many families you will find an old hag in the background who hurries the baby round to the church, often without consent or knowledge of the parents.' The font is not the major factor in the advance or retreat of religion in Russia.

The vital battleground is the school.

Soviet children go to school at seven, and some to a primary school at five. The leaving age has been raised from fourteen to fifteen, 1964 being the year by which every Soviet child is to receive eight years compulsory education. The most able continue for another three years to reach the eleventh and highest grade and leave at eighteen.[1] Eight years is enough to give a thorough grounding in Communist, materialist outlook.

Atheism is not in the curriculum as a subject, in the manner that Divinity or Scripture generally appears in Western schools, but it hovers in the background. 'Teaching should be organized,' runs an article in *Sovetskaya Estoniya* of October 23rd 1963, 'so that every lesson in any subject should help to form the ideology of the schoolchildren.' This policy is often ignored. As the senior lecturer at a Pedagogical Institute near Bryansk wrote in January 1964, 'some teachers instead of unmasking religious ravings shy at the very mention of God'.

A teacher who is keen will constantly make atheist points. In history lessons the Orthodox Church's opposition to the Revolution will be emphasized. In chemistry an experiment to prove the components of bread will evoke a gibe at the doctrine of the eucharist, and as late as December 1963, long years after monks of the Orthodox Church had abandoned the trick-miracles which played on the credulity of Tsarist *muzhiks*, a chemistry teacher in No. 37 School at Tallin was happily explaining 'in an intelligible way how ministers of the Church making use of the achievements of chemistry deceive believers by various "miracles" and arrange the "self-renewal" of icons, church domes and crosses'. In biology and natural science 'the churchmen's myths about the divine creation of man and everything living on earth are exposed'. A lesson on astronomy refers to Galileo's persecution by the Inquisition. An introduction to the marvels of flight and space exploration will produce the comment, 'Religion first forbade any thought that man could fly.' This curious statement is based on a story of the father of the Wright brothers, a Presbyterian minister, who is said to have remarked in 1875 (when they were small boys)

[1] The Soviet School is divided by years into grades (the word is sometimes translated 'forms'.) A First Grader is aged 7–8, a Sixth Former is aged 12–13 and so on.

that the idea of flying was blasphemous! If the views of such an obscure individual may topple God from His throne there is no reason why He should not be put back again by reflection that Leonardo da Vinci not only painted the sublime *Last Supper* but also designed a flying machine . . . The whole argument is silly.

The force does not lie in such childish points, but in the all-pervasive environment of school, the assumption of a materialistic universe, of the absurdity of religious belief. Unless acquainted with a Christian home, Soviet schoolchildren never attend divine service, read or hear about God except in a negative sense. It is taken for granted and drummed into them that the educated, cultured, progressive person has no religion, which is for the elderly and uncultured.

That is not enough. In April 1963 the R.S.F.S.R. Education Minister wrote that 'we do not want our boys and girls to grow up merely ignorant of religious questions. We want them to become convinced, militant atheists.' *Science and Religion* complained in December that: 'In the overwhelming majority of cases the theoretical store of the seventeen-year-old is confined to the completely just but unsubstantiated statement: "God does not exist." ' In 1958 a special course in 'The Fundamentals of Scientific Atheism' was introduced to higher educational institutes. It is optional in the R.S.F.S.R., compulsory in the Ukraine and Lithuania. The students regarded it 'as a tenth-rate subject and have a poor attendance at lectures'. Yet the course is vital, *Komsomolskaya Pravda* has urged, because of 'the very interesting character of religious preaching in the churches'. Early in 1964 the Party announced that Chairs of Scientific Atheism were to be established in certain universities and pedagogical institutes.

. . . . .

A great many schoolchildren, from homes where religion has been smothered a generation, swallow the atheist attitude, slogans and all, as is shown in a delightful letter received by the Far East Broadcasting Company during June 1963 from a seventeen-year-old boy: 'HELLO! I am a high school student (11th grade). I openly denounce you on behalf of Soviet Youth. Your hysterical pronouncements about god are useless. Would you not be better off, if you were to stop them? They do not bring the desired results anyway. Your priests are rotten with dishonesty. What can you say, you, the weak descendants of the bourgeoisie? If you have the rebuttal, you can forward it to the following address . . .'

A growing minority of Soviet Youth, however, come from believing homes, and thus from the day they first hear anti-religious fairy tales at primary school are subjected to tension: at home taught to pray at mother's knee, at school taught no God exists; at home learning that all things bright and beautiful are given by a loving Creator, at school told Christ is laughingly mythical and religion an evil deception. Parents have the legal right to instruct their children in religion at home, and a large number of teachers are genuinely careful neither to interfere with this parental freedom nor to 'insult the feelings of believers', especially in families of priests and pastors.

The official attitude deplores such sensitivity. 'Imagine what happens,' said a Moscow broadcaster in July 1963, 'in those cases where the school and family act on the child from different ideo-logical and spiritual points of view.' Broadcasts and articles con-tinually attack the 'harm done to young children by religious instruction at home'. The Party line knows nothing of a little child's wondering trust in a heavenly Father, a child's instinct of adoration; to a Communist, a small boy or girl will be religious only by parental pressure or brute force. A religious child must by definition be unhappy, repressed, retarded, 'a moral cripple'—the phrase comes again and again. 'It is incumbent on the school to fight so that the children of religious parents shall not grow up into moral cripples but into real builders of Communism and fully developed people.'

The Miraculous Icon has a passage in which the crusading atheist schoolmistress calls such parents 'social criminals'. 'My pupil learns one thing at school, and the opposite at home. Either the school will educate him to deny God or his family will bring him up as a double-faced hypocrite. There can be no compromise. Let the parents believe whatever they like. But the future of the children does not belong only to them. Parents like that are social criminals . . . There are many crimes which are not defined in any particular paragraph of the law. But that does not make them any less harmful for society.' A writer in *Molodoi Kom-munist* (*Young Communist*) a few years back was yet more venomous. He wanted such parents in the dock. 'In religious families the standards of the human dignity of the child are trampled on in the most shameless manner, its feelings, thoughts and will are outraged . . . Surely the open and secret tears of the children call for stern punishment.'

A Western reader may be growing confused by this talk of '*moral* cripples' and 'outraged human dignity'. He can under-stand a Soviet schoolmaster dismissing religious parents as un-enlightened, backward or deceived, but why *immoral*?

To Communists this is the crux of the matter. They maintain that a child is a moral cripple unless growing up to be a 'new Communist man', self-sufficient, proud, scornful of meekness, head held high in the manner of W. E. Henley's 'I am the master of my fate, I am the captain of my soul', and Swinburne's 'Glory to Man in the highest! for Man is the master of things.' Because the Christian kneels he must be a miserable creature; because he owns a Master he must be a cringing slave: 'A pickpocket takes a man's money or his watch, a bandit inflicts a mortal wound, a burglar steals all the valuables in a house. But the "brothers and sisters in Christ" distort a man's very mind, steal everything from him, deflect him from happiness in life to dreams of bliss after death and kill his pride and his confidence in his own powers.' The Communist is a stranger to the spiritual secret learned by Paul and countless Christians since, 'When I am weak, then am I strong,' to the truth expressed in the old hymn:

> *Make me a captive, Lord,*
> *And then I shall be free;*
> *Force me to render up my sword,*
> *And I shall conq'ror be.*

The Communist stifles the deep-rooted human instinct which Augustine expressed: 'Our hearts are restless until they rest in Thee,' and bends his energies to produce 'Communist man'.

In this the Party youth organizations play the primary role, from the day the child becomes, at the age of seven, a Little Octo-brist and goes on to be a Pioneer wearing the red three-pointed scarf. Membership is not, in theory, compulsory, though there are increasing instances where a child has been enrolled against the parents' wish or its own. A child who is not a Pioneer will miss much of the fun of camps, games and social activities, and be damaged in school career. Membership of the Komsomol (for youths aged 14–28) is, on the other hand, more selective.

Many Baptist parents permit their children to become Little Octobrists and Pioneers, conscious that isolation may be more hurtful than indoctrination. There must be cases of children forbidden the Pioneers who grow up to be Party members and atheists, just as there are many Pioneers who reach manhood or womanhood strong Christians.

.   .   .   .

Wherever school and Party organizations take their task seriously the small child is pressed into the accepted mould. 'Twenty children in sectarian bondage—that was a blot on the school. A fight for each one began,' tells a village headmaster from the Chechen-Ingush Autonomous Republic. The different teachers each concentrated on two, 'and thus every little "pray-baby" got his good guide—a teacher whose task it was to drag him out of the sectarian bog into which the children, thanks to their parents, had already put a foot'.

Where a Christian couple are determined to prevent atheist indoctrination, and teachers or Party equally determined the other way, stronger measures are used: the parents can be deprived of parental rights and the children sent to be brought up in a State Home or in an 'Internat', one of the new boarding-schools. Deprivation of parental rights is becoming lamentably frequent. Or custody can be given to another member of the family. A case occurred in Leningrad in June 1963.

Mrs. Lyubov Vasilevna Mikryukova had become a Baptist in 1942 after the death of her first husband at the front. She and her second husband, a Baptist like herself, had nine young children. Every evening they had devotions with singing, Bible reading and, in the Baptist manner, brief extempore prayer round the family starting with the youngest who could pray, ending with Papa. Baptist friends frequently called for hymn-singing sessions.

The Mikryukovs were very unworldly. Moreover, they would not let the older children join the Pioneers, and although in some such instances the boys or girls share their parents' convictions, Lyuba and Vera seem to have harboured deep resentment. When Mrs. Mikryukova's only son by her first marriage, Robert Malozemov, a handsome, fair-haired fellow of twenty-three or four, returned from the Army the family tore apart. Robert, a 'merry and effervescent Komsomol', was a flaming atheist, 'a really talented anti-religious worker', so Secretary Ilichev called him. He began a 'painful struggle for the souls of his young brothers and sisters'. He took them to the puppet theatre and circus, he openly ridiculed the faith of his mother and step-father, and the elder girls sided with him while the little ones, enjoying the puppets but loving their parents, were in a tug-of-war of tensions in the overcrowded little apartment.

Robert, determined to wrest his step-brother and sister 'from the black net of the Baptists and to bring them up as real Soviet people', played his trump card. He applied to the People's Court for custody, telling a lurid story of the children cowering in terror under beds while the Baptists sang! He said his step-father thrice tore out the wires of his radio (possibly he had turned it on loud during family prayers) and threatened to smash his new television set. When some of the children sided with him his mother (he claimed) shouted that she should no longer feed or clothe them. Each day thenceforth Robert would 'prepare dinner, feed the youngsters, clean their clothes and help with their lessons', before leaving for night shift at the works.

Robert and *Sovetskaya Rossiya*, which described the case, cannot have it both ways.

The parents were given as Baptists, not as of some underworld perversion of Christianity, yet apparently behaved as no Baptists do except in the columns of a Soviet newspaper. They were described in court as sitting silent, 'and their piercing eyes burn with fearsome malice'—as is usual in the papers. Their one reported intervention was the mother's self-centred, 'I am suffering for my faith.' Unless the newspaper suppressed their testimony, they were given no opportunity of defence.

Robert won custody of the six elder children, and a

maintenance order at the parents' expense until they should come of age.

His photograph appeared in *Sovetskaya Rossiya* in June with five of them—the sixth had a cold. On New Year's Day 1964 the photogenic Robert was in *Leningradskaya Pravda*, with the children feeding at a jolly feast probably provided by the paper. The two older girls look as merry as Robert. The others look as if thoughts may often stray to Mama and Papa, and to the three babies on whom Robert also has designs.

CHAPTER XVI

WHY INNA, VITALY AND ROZA HELD
THEIR BREATH

'OUR families are divided. That is one of our problems,' say the Baptists, for middle-aged or elderly may have both atheists and believers among their grown-up offspring. The Baptists say too: 'Our children go through an unbelieving stage'; most parents do not regret this, being free at least of that forced product of an over-religious home or school, the excessively pious child who grows into an insipid or antagonistic adult. The child of Christian parents in Russia must reach faith the hard way.

In some schools the path may be less rugged, for children are often as bored by anti-God agitation as are their elders. 'When pupils in senior classes are invited to join a circle on atheism,' wrote a headmaster of Vilnius in Lithuania in *Sovetskaya Litva*, November 22nd 1963, 'they at times shrug their shoulders in perplexity. "Why? I am after all a non-believer." When you explain that a circle of atheism consists precisely of unbelievers and its task is to fight for those in whom survivals of the past still remain, you get the answer that this is of no interest at all to him, the pupil, and let others occupy themselves with it.' The headmaster feared that these indifferent adolescents were the very stuff of future converts to religion. Moreover, in the less intellectually regimented atmosphere of the 'sixties young people are reported to be opposed to an unquestioning rejection of religion, much as their counterparts in the West reject its unquestioning acceptance.

Open advocacy of Christ is extraordinarily hard for a Soviet adolescent.

On the afternoon of April 10th 1963 Moscow Home Service broadcast a recording of a debate arranged at Moscow School No. 500 among senior boys and girls who had been reading a story, by the author of *The Miraculous Icon*, about a sixteen-year-old girl in the tenth form of a Soviet school who believed in God.

The debate was lively, several girls maintaining that religious belief arose from lack of education, and a youth contradicting them: 'Believers are not only children and old people, and it is quite incorrect to say that the priests are uneducated . . .'

A little later a man, probably a master, spoke: 'No one can know whether there are believers in the school or not. But it is obvious there are cowards!'

Sensation.

The man went on: 'An anonymous note has been passed round which says: "You need not believe in God, but I do." The writer of that note had better come forward and defend his point of view!'

Silence.

'No one has come forward!'

Loud laughter.

If the anonymous note-writer is to be condemned as a secret disciple by those who sit at ease in lands of religious freedom they should reflect on his considerable courage. Had he (or she) come forward at a debate being recorded for radio his name would be branded publicly, and he could expect consequent difficulty in getting a job, or securing entry to a higher educational institute on leaving school shortly. His views, however ably expressed, would be subjected to catch questions by the trained atheist agitator present (a member of the district Komsomol's atheist headquarters) and by his own schoolmasters; and he could be certain that before the debate went over the air his contribution would be edited to appear ineffectual or ludicrous, unless the policy of Moscow Radio changed miraculously overnight. Yet he circulated a note, risking exposure. Among the thousands in other schools who heard the broadcast, here and there a Christian would have been heartened.

That particular broadcast was intended for Komsomols (Young Communist Leaguers). Membership of the Komsomol is an almost essential requirement for the making of a successful career, even in sport: few if any of the Soviet athletes at the Olympic Games of 1964 would not be members. And atheism is built into its constitution. Plenty of Komsomols are violent atheists like Robert, who 'rescued' his Baptist step-brothers and sisters; the majority will at least be careful to parade the appropriate sentiments and slogans on demand.

A patriotic, socially alert Christian who wishes to join the activities of the nation's senior youth organization is placed in an invidious position. The story of a Moscow boy called Sasha Turkin neatly illustrates the dilemma.

Sasha Turkin, seventeen, of School No. 147, applied for membership of the Young Communist League. In the customary manner his application was read out before the Komsomols of his class, who could blackball it. By *Komsomolskaya Pravda*'s version of events, 'They began to question him on his knowledge of the Y.C.L. Statutes. Sasha answered the way he answered classroom questions, slowly and confidently. Everyone was ready to vote him in, when Vitaly Bouzhenko rose. "Do you believe in God?" he asked.

'Class 10a froze for a moment, and then a hum of indignation arose: What a silly question!

'Vitaly, who had asked it in jest, wanted to change the subject, but Sasha said quietly:

' "Yes, I do."

'Inna Levshina's cheeks flamed. It was she who had recommended Sasha for membership. Viktor Kalin stared at Sasha; two years ago they had shared a double desk in the classroom. Roza Trepalina, the Y.C.L. organizer, stunned, kept silent. Could this be? Sasha, whom everyone seemed to know so well—Sasha, who had stood confidently at the blackboard and outlined the Darwinian theory . . . Did this Sasha believe in God?'

According to the newspaper the horrid fact had never occurred to Sasha's schoolmates. He had been one of the best in the class, earning high grades, excellent reports term by term. 'They looked at Sasha with tremendous surprise as if they had never seen him before. Suddenly someone's voice came from the rear seats:

' "Nonsense! He doesn't believe in God, he is just saying that. Let's vote!"

'Inna, Vitaly and Roza caught their breath. Of course it was nonsense! Of course it couldn't be!

'Sasha Turkin was unanimously admitted to membership in the Y.C.L.'

137

The newspaper was distressed that 'the Young Communists did not see Sasha as their ideological antagonist'. It presumed Sasha had been forced to believe by his father. 'It was from him that Sasha first heard of God. Amazed, he tried to argue. But before him stood his father, with unquestionable authority on his side.' *Komsomolskaya Pravda* seems to have forgotten that Sasha had heard about God long before he was of an age to argue; and his quiet affirmation of belief, 'Yes, I do,' does not suggest a timorous father-ridden hypocrite.

The whole story undoubtedly had a spice of editorial imagination. Sasha's classmates probably knew all along that their popular, brainy pal was a believer. Vitaly did not ask his question in joke but because he was anti-religious. The others sided with Sasha and could no more see why he should not have a hand in shaping the nation's future, despite the Statute bidding Komsomols be militant atheists, than Sasha could see, as the newspaper admitted, 'his Y.C.L. classmates as militant atheists and ideological fighters. He knew that he would not have to give up his views, to reconsider his convictions.'

The school Komsomol committee confirmed Sasha's application after a few perfunctory questions about his belief, and the town bureau of the Young Communist League, the Party officials in charge of Komsomol affairs, to whom once again Sasha attested, 'I believe in God,' gave him his membership card. 'We can't refuse to accept him because of one phrase. "I believe in God,"' remarked the secretary—and at that the newspaper really was shocked. It criticized class, school and town bureau for surrendering ideological convictions. Above all, it blamed Sasha for not facing 'the dilemma, either Y.C.L. or God'.

Was Sasha wrong? He knew that he never could be a candidate for Party membership (and certainly not be elected), for that implied a deliberate atheism; no Christian can be a full-blooded Communist in the Soviet Union. To Sasha and his classmates the Young Communist League was a channel of patriotism rather than of ideological 'correctness', a cheerful amalgam of, as it were, Boy Scouts, Girl Guides and a hikers club.

.   .   .   .

The whole dilemma of Christian and Komsomol was mirrored in a peculiarly painful way by a letter which *Komsomolskaya Pravda* printed on December 20th 1963 because the writer seemed a possible convert to atheism.

He was a twenty-two-year-old Moldavian, who wrote that his parents were Evangelical Christians/Baptists. 'From my earliest years they taught me to pray to God and to love my neighbour as myself. When I went to school, nobody hindered me from learning. On the contrary, my father helped me and punished me for carelessness.' When a senior the boy read books and went to the cinema. 'My father did not forbid me to do this either and always only warned me that I should conduct myself decently. At school I was very interested in astronomy and chemistry.'

He did not join the Komsomol, 'because I knew that there was no place for me there; you see I believe in God and go to meetings of believers and everyone in our village knew this very well'. When he was called up he did excellently in the Army because he did not smoke, drink or swear ('I am not boasting, but I am telling the truth'). Officers and fellow-soldiers respected him.

In the Army he naturally had joined the Komsomol, and it had since meant much to him. What was he then to do? 'I have still got a grain of faith in God.' He could not bear to leave the Komsomol, yet to deny God and turn atheist would be to betray his mother's deathbed wish and 'my conscience will torture me all my life'.

He asked the newspaper for advice. But he did not give his name, because if his Komsomol comrades heard of his doubts 'every type of explanatory work will begin'. He knew what 'individual work with believers' could be like.

Pressure increases as a youth or girl grows older, for by seventeen or eighteen faith cannot be dismissed as a consequence of domineering parents.

Valentine Murarova, who lived in a coal-mining village in the Donets Basin of the Ukraine, was about to enter an art school, with hopes of a higher institute afterwards. Just then she became a Baptist—and did not reach the art school. Instead, the Party organization at the pit set a Communist on her 'to help Valentina find the correct path in life. He put her to drawing placards, diagrams and slogans. According to *Kommunist Ukrainy* (June 1963), this wise treatment bred 'a feeling of self-respect and faith in her own abilities . . . and her need to seek an illusory happiness vanished'. Atheist heart-to-heart talks enabled her 'to break finally with religion and find her place in life'. Valentina has probably found a place in the art school too.

There is no reasonable doubt from evidence which trickles out that Christian youth is discriminated against in the allotment of coveted places in institutes and universities, although an outstanding brain would almost certainly be accepted; his political education would be intensified. *Science and Religion* also admits cases, claiming them isolated, 'when on various pretexts but essentially for the same reason, students in senior classes who have committed no offence and have been making entirely satisfactory progress, have been expelled from their higher educational establishments'. In the summer of 1963 a girl at the Moscow Engineering and Economics Institute was ostracized and later expelled because a believer. And the 'twenty-three-year-old son of the regent of the Baptist community' of Frunze in Central Asia, a footwear worker, had a rough time at the technical evening institute when students and teachers decided to help him out of his darkness. They bombarded him with questions, made him see an anti-God film, told him to read atheist Bible commentaries and parodies. He has been an able, regular student until this persecution, which not unnaturally induced a reluctance to attend classes, and more time spent teaching the Baptist youth group, which met in private houses. After an evening at the institute at which he suffered particularly unwelcome attentions he resigned. And was miserable. He wanted technical education, wanted to do well. Swallowing his pride, he sought to withdraw his resignation. The director told him it was for his works collective to decide. A meeting was called which 'became a real atheistic tribune'. They grilled him for five hours and Aleksandr would not apostatize. Like Luther his attitude was 'Here I stand. I can no other.' The collective refused to recommend his reacceptance.

More young men and women are dismissed from institutes because they are believers, or find entry closed, than *Science and Religion* cares to admit. Nevertheless, in a vast country which sets much store on higher education there are very many still receiving it, and the higher the institute, the more anomalous, in Party eyes, is an unrecanted Christian among its students. The Party, as always, blames ineffective agitation. That two sisters in Latvia, the one nearly qualified as a doctor, the other a graduate from a school of assistant doctors, should both be strong Baptists, was featured in the local paper in November 1963 as proof of the rotten standard of anti-religious work.

·   ·   ·   ·

Among Soviet youth, as in other sectors of the nation, the Christian faith not only refuses to die; it is virile.

When the R.S.F.S.R. Deputy Minister of Education went to the microphone on October 19th 1963 he had to report: 'In Krasnoyarsk, schoolchildren of the fifth to ninth classes[1] of the local schools attend the secret prayer meetings of the Pentecostals. The same thing can be seen also at the prayer meetings of the Baptists in Omsk region. Some sects, in order to attract schoolchildren, use such methods as children's choirs. Thus, in six Baptist communities in Bryansk children's choirs have been organized, composed of ten to fifteen members, etc. Moreover, they are directed by young believers who are under eighteen years of age. In Perm the Baptist community has a choral group which comprises more than twenty-five children and adolescents. And how many schoolchildren in towns and villages still go to church!'

Local Christians need courage and tact, for the law is against them. Of one city in Central Asia it was reported that 'the Baptist leaders were not afraid of infringing the Soviet laws relating to worship. They organized Bible courses for young people, which were attended by 50 pupils between 16 and 18 years of age. Afterwards they were all baptized. And their schoolteachers, with unpardonable timidity, saw all this going on and did not consider it necessary to interfere.' In a town of the same region pastor and helpers organized games and hikes and bathing parties and Bible classes.

The full story of the revolt of Russian youth against blind atheism cannot yet be told.

[1] i.e. between the ages of eleven and sixteen.

141

CHAPTER XVII

WHERE ARE THE CATACOMBS?

MUCH of the Baptist offensive in industry, the professions, the schools, would be impossible were the sect wholly proscribed, not led by a body with legal standing in the State, the All-Union Council of Evangelical Christians/Baptists.

Many evangelical believers distrust this council.

One of the sharpest tragedies for Christians in the U.S.S.R. is the tension between those convinced that the road ahead lies between the high, prickly hedges of obedience to an Atheist State and those who deplore compromise with the Anti-Christ.

Many Orthodox churchmen refuse to acknowledge the authority of certain dignitaries who appear over-willing agents of the Soviet Government. Among Baptists the tension is strong too. In most congregations are men and women impatient with their leaders' willingness to accept limitations, or puzzled that discrimination is not resisted and irksome laws ignored; or convinced that the Council renders unto Caesar considerably more than the things that are Caesar's. The Baptist Congress of 1963 warned believers in strongest terms against such 'dangerous and damaging' people. And beyond the congregations which acknowledge the Council are those who reject it; an amorphous multitude of clandestine sects and churches which cannot be numbered, whether by groups or individual membership, being unrecognized and therefore unregistered. It shades off into the lunatic fringe traditional to Russia, but this submerged multitude contains much that is true, honest, just, pure and lovely, though not, in the circumstances, of good report. And out of it came the Thirty Two Siberians.

·   ·   ·   ·

Are the Baptist leaders what the West calls fellow-travellers, collaborators in the wartime, dishonourable sense? Some Westerners and exiled Russians equate the Council with Hitler's servile church in Nazi Germany, and find the true 'Confessing Church' among the unregistered groups, the spirit of first-century Christianity only with those who repudiate the Soviet way of life, to endure in the catacombs—or in prison.

No man not a Soviet Christian has earned, by suffering, the right to adjudicate in this grievous dispute.

It may perhaps be surmised that the Baptist leaders believe a little freedom better than none. Co-operation with the authorities enables them to minister to the spiritual needs of the flock; if they must walk in a strait-jacket they can at least walk, and walk forward, strengthening and encouraging the Church instead of lying impotent and silent. Were they to accede to the demands of followers that the atheist State should be 'testified against', prayer-houses would close, the Gospel would be stifled. The leaders take full advantage also of Soviet desire to retain a show-case of religious freedom for the world's eyes. The link with Churches beyond the U.S.S.R. is highly precious to Christians in Russia. If Baptist and Orthodox leaders refused to abide by the State's view of what may or may not be said abroad, or to foreign visitors, this link would be broken. The Orthodox go farther than the Baptists in promoting the Soviet image overseas, but the view that they and the Baptists joined the World Council of Churches to be Russian troublemakers does not accord with the intensity of desire for hands and hearts across the sea—and across the Iron Curtain—or with their words and attitude at World Council meetings.

Willingness to obey the State springs from motives deeper than a diplomacy that may sheer into time-serving. The Baptist leaders believe their policy to be in tune with Scripture: 'Every person must submit to the supreme authorities. There is no authority but by act of God, and the existing authorities are instituted by him; consequently anyone who rebels against authority is resisting a divine institution, and those who so resist have themselves to thank for the punishment they will receive. What Paul wrote of pagan Rome the Baptists apply to atheist Soviet Russia. The Apostle Peter bade the early Christians submit themselves to every ordinance of man for the Lord's sake, to honour a depraved Emperor worshipped by the State as divine, who shortly would send Christians in their hundreds to be nailed to crosses, thrown to wild beasts or burned alive. And at the last, after varying degrees of toleration spiced at times with violent persecution, Christianity won the conflict—after three centuries . . . Communism has not been in power fifty years.

The analogy is not too inapt, for the Early Church had no quarrel with Roman imperial sway as such, though they lived for the day when the kingdoms of this world should become the kingdoms of Christ. Most of the Russian Baptist leaders admire the Soviet social system and regard its atheism as an extraneous component which at length, if they remain faithful, will be jettisoned. 'We are grateful to England,' one of them said suddenly with a nod to me as we sat drinking. *borsch*, the meaty Ukrainian soup, 'for her two great gifts to Russia. The Bible Society, which gave us the Bible in Russian, and Karl Marx, who gave us our social system!' The idea that Christians are a fifth column longing to overturn the Revolution is far astray. Marxism has become, as the young poet Yevgeny Yevtushenko has written, 'a part of the Russian people's flesh and blood'; the more so that they may now laugh a little at its mistakes, grumble at its irritations and indulge in more private enterprise on the side.

'Many of us can still remember the old, obsolete, backward, ignorant Russia.' In memory or in history they look back to the Tsarist era when they were 'slaves', the grim enough reality being embroidered by time and textbooks. The fearful sufferings of early Soviet decades, the famines and the Purge are written off as the price of progress. Miseries and shortages which were thrust on Russia by the German invasion give point to the general impression that conditions improve yearly thanks to a benevolent government.

Russians naturally feel tremendous pride in sputniks, luniks and Soviet technical achievements. Mr. Khrushchev has their affection and trust. They have lived so long in a strange pressurized world in which all news is doctored and slanted that most of them take at face value the perpetual slogans. Whatever Stalin meant by 'Peace', whatever Khrushchev means, the plain Russian has no doubt that as one of them put it, 'The worst peace is better than war.' The plain Russian who is not clever enough to read between the lines of his turgid daily newspaper really does believe, or nearly believe, all about wicked imperialists and Western war-mongers, really does believe, or nearly believe, that his brother toiler in England and America is groaning under the heel of a bloated plutocracy.[1]

When a Baptist presbyter said, 'We are grateful to our government,' he meant it.

'But do you not,' I asked, 'long for the time when there will be Christians in the government of Russia?'

'Oh *yes*, we do! We pray for it every day!'

.   .   .   .

Those who are unhappy with the Council's respect for State-imposed limitations, and, as the Baptist leaders say, 'do not understand the conditions of the times and introduce differences of opinion among our brotherhood', are found both within the congregations and operating illegally outside.

The line between recognized (if unregistered) congregations and the unnumbered mass of illegal Christians is drawn thin; groups may sometimes be one side, sometimes the other. Differences do not concern politics alone. Some Pentecostalists did not acknowledge the Union with Baptists in 1945. Others broke later because Baptist leaders frowned upon 'speaking in tongues', that strange manifestation which Pentecostalists cherish, which Soviet authorities hate, and the Churches of classical tradition in the West ignored or mocked—until its recent appearance in staid Protestant Episcopalian circles of California and, to a smaller extent, in certain Anglican congregations in England. Forty thousand eastern Ukrainian Pentecostalists are reported to have withdrawn from the Union,[2] thus placing themselves outside the law. Other groups of evangelicals reject union because, like Independents of old, they will not call any man master save God alone.

Nevertheless, refusal for conscience sake to obey the Anti-Christ, the Communists, is deep rooted and widespread. The All-

[1] An English-speaking Baptist waved a *Daily Worker* (the only British newspaper on sale in the U.S.S.R.) and said happily, 'This is what we read when we want news of Britain.' I told him it was like reading a paper about Baptists edited by Roman Catholics!

[2] The figures are from Pentecostal sources, given in *Pentecost*, March 1957.

Union Council's call that 'We Christians must co-operate with our people and adopt a sensible attitude towards the common problems of our country, help to solve them, and do everything we can to promote the welfare of the Soviet people' is rejected as a call to aid and succour those who have forsaken God's covenant, thrown down His altars and slain His prophets with the sword. Obedience to God's commands is the over-riding compulsion.

Eleanor Lipper, a German-born woman eleven years in Stalin's labour camps, has a moving story of a 'dark complexioned, dark-eyed peasant woman with shining black hair, who always radiated cheerfulness and kindness, whose strong beautiful body not even camp life could afflict'. Nadya, in her late thirties, came from some sect in the Ukraine. At the end of her sentence she was reunited unexpectedly with her husband, whom prison experience had broken, and they were kept, released but in exile, on a collective-farm in the Far East. Nadya refused to work on Sundays or holy days. She was rebuked, warned, threatened with prosecution. 'Sobbing, her husband went on his knees and pleaded with her: "Nadya, I implore you, Nadya, give in. This sin cannot be counted against us because we are not committing it voluntarily. Nadya, have mercy on yourself, on me. I no longer have the strength to go through all that horror again."'

'"You do what God has given you strength to do," she said softly in her melodious Ukrainian accent, "and I must do what my conscience tells me to do."'

Three weeks later Nadya rejoined Eleanor Lipper in the prison camp. 'Her powerful arms embraced us, her large eyes examined our wasted faces with sorrowful affection.

'"Nadya, what did you get?"

'"Five years," she said in a calm, indifferent voice, putting her bundle down on the boards of a bedstead.'

Nadya's sect may not have been of evangelical origin. The Soviet authorities now tend to call all such people Pentecostalist, and take pains to besmirch that name. If reports of court cases in the early nineteen-sixties are taken at face value Russian Pentecostalists behave utterly unlike their brethren elsewhere in the world, being not only enthusiasts but grim, harsh, violent and malevolent.

146

The words of an unbeliever present at a 'Pentecostal' meeting, 'some rolled on the floor in convulsions beating themselves, while others, with a stupid, vacant expression on their faces, stared into the distance and uttered inarticulate cries', do not make too unfair a description of 'Holy Rollers', in Russia or elsewhere. The refusal of certain Soviet 'Pentecostalists' to possess radios or television sets is not unexpected, being known among religious extremists in Britain and America, as is also exclusion of intercourse with fellow humans not of precisely similar persuasion. If in the U.S.S.R. this proscription extends to cups and plates used by 'unbelievers' that conforms with traditions embedded in the wilder shores of ancient Russian religion. If 'Pentecostalists' are said to drive men and women mad religious hysteria appears throughout the world, and in the tensions of a land where virulent atheists and bigoted religionists pull a soul back and forth, an unstable personality may be toppled into mental disorder.

Unfortunately for Soviet propaganda there is evidence that incarceration in a mental home has been used by Communists as a means of persuading or silencing men or women who are sane by every standard but that of an unyielding atheist. And when 'Pentecostalists' are further said to thieve, embezzle and even incite to murder and suicide the detached observer is at once confused and blinded by the impossibility of sorting truth from deliberate misrepresentation.

CHAPTER XVIII

BEYOND THE LAW

Two men in their thirties, Nikolai Filippovich Voloshin and Ivan Fedotov, both now in prison, have received nation-wide notoriety as most abominable, bestial religious fanatics.

Voloshin got five years in prison in 1945 at the age of twenty for 'desertion from the Soviet Forces'—which could mean he was a conscientious objector. Released in 1950, in 1955 he was sentenced to ten years for embezzlement and cruelty. Embezzlement would be the obvious charge against the leader of an illegal sect whose followers gave him gifts to support his ministry, and he certainly travelled widely, for adherents of his 'Children of God' have been reported as far apart as Moscow and a distant part of Kazakhstan. Cruelty, if a criminal charge, would lie easily against a man who sought to heal the sick by prayer and faith, forbade the services of a doctor.

After only two years Voloshin was released by an amnesty of 1957 and soon was leading his followers in all-night vigils in woods near Moscow. Even the Communists admit that he preached a Gospel of love ('saturated with unction and kindness . . .') and high morals, but he preached that Christians should not join trades unions, attend factory meetings, competitions or any entertainments, nor take part in State holidays because they honoured victories of the Anti-Christ. When a woman follower died of purulent appendicitis after Voloshin had told her family to depend on prayer the militia were on his trail. In 1961 Voloshin received five years from Ryazan Provincial Court.

Ivan Fedotov had played in the football team of his region and served in the Red Army. He had once been a Baptist. He was given ten years in 1961 as indirectly responsible for two suicides and for incitement to murder: he is said to have urged a follower to kill her little daughter as expiation after missing prayer meetings and allowing her to attend Pioneer camp; the murder was forestalled by friends.

.   .   .   .

Whatever the truth about Voloshin and Fedotov, now doing hard labour in some remote camp in the frozen north or the Virgin Lands, whether they are defamed disciples conscious of Christ's presence in their distress or diseased minds eaten up by a god of their own invention, a lunatic fringe certainly exists in Soviet Russia, formed by lineal or spiritual descendants of peculiar zealots of Tsarist times.

Alongside mild, nonconforming Molokans in Transcaucasia, including young men and women who combine Komsomol membership with psalm singing and the old Molokan traditions, are 'Shakers', who could stem by some tortuous route from the Shakers of the United States but more likely derive from older pseudo-Orthodox groups. A young 'prophetess' was gaoled after a six-day trial at Novosibirsk, Central Siberia, in February 1962. There are Murashkovites, alleged to drink eucharists of human blood; and Innocentists and the 'True Orthodox Church' and shadowy followers of the Romanovs.

A ghastly incident of the attempted crucifixion of a woman in 1957 would seem an echo of the pre-Revolutionary Khlysts (Flagellants)—if it happened. Komsomols in a village of the Semi-palatinsk region said they were returning one evening from a meeting when they heard yells. They burst open the door of Yakov Stadel's house and found his young wife Olga half naked, 'standing by a high white cross; there were people around shouting excitedly and waving their arms'. Yakov and his twenty-seven-year-old friend Andrei Dering held nails and a heavy hammer. 'The savages were about to nail the young woman to the cross.' Yakov was sentenced to ten years, Andrei to seven. According to a film based on the incident, Olga broke with the sect.

If the Komsomols interrupted a ritual they may have misunderstood its meaning. No murder or physical suffering need have been intended, but an acted, symbolic expiation of sins, however

149

deranged and frantic. Olga Stadel's crucifixion, however, has been worked to the limit in anti-sectarian propaganda, and typifies the thorns thrown in the path of genuine Christianity in Russia by the anarchy of heresies which, while Soviet repression continues, will fester here and there throughout the nation.

Nor are all these heresies ancient. Jehovah's Witnesses have spread like wildfire in Russia, especially since the end of the Second World War. Jehovists, as the Russians call them, whose disruptive tendencies, persistence, and bland application of Christian terms to totally unChristian meanings have not endeared them to the historic Churches throughout the world, enrage the Soviet authorities. Jehovah's Witnesses are opposed to all governments, most of whom treat them as somewhat a joke. The Soviet Government treat them as a deadly serious threat, aggravated by their being a closely organized world network with headquarters at Brooklyn, New York, a name printed openly on all the literature which they smuggle in and distribute with quite extraordinary aplomb. In the eyes of the Kremlin Jehovists are spies, imperialist agents, almost a subsidiary of the State Department.

'Where did the Jehovah's Witnesses' Literature that you were distributing come from?' asked the judge in Ryshkani, Moldavia, at a trial in August 1963.

'From overseas,' replied the prisoner, Ivan Zaporozhan.

'It was anti-Soviet?'

'Yes.'

'Do you admit that you were acting in a criminal way?'

'I not only admit it, but I condemn it, and I am breaking with this underground business once and for all. I regret having wasted my youth, that eighteen years of my life have gone for nothing ...'

Since Zaporozhan, who had been in prison previously on refusing military service, had renounced the sect, the judge let him off with three years probation, during which a suspended sentence of ten years would hang over him. The Prosecutor hoped the other Jehovists in court (who had not been arrested, presumably having not been caught distributing *The Watchtower*) would understand that 'membership of this reactionary organization is a crime against the fatherland and the people'.

The newspaper reporting the case, *Sovetskaya Moldaviya,*

implied that all 'brother and sisters in Christ' stood under the same condemnation.

·　　　·　　　·　　　·

Also largely beyond the law are the Adventists.

Russia has been a seed-bed of Adventists for generations, humble suffering folk comforting their minds by peering into a future when their warfare shall be accomplished, and the crooked shall be made straight, and the rough places plain, and the glory of the Lord shall be revealed. Visions and prophecies have flashed across the Russian scene from time immemorial, as prophets and seers, earnest or deluded, gathered the poor and oppressed around them deep in the forests, or in far-away huts on the steppes when the snow lies firm and the skies are grey. This Advent hope has never been so strong as in the fifth decade of the Communist era.

The Seventh Day Adventists are an officially recognized sect numbering about 30,000. Like the Baptists, they have off-shoots who do not accept the leadership of the registered body. There are also many groups of Christians unrelated to the S.D.A.'s and not accepting their distinctive teachings, who are loosely termed Adventists, and are akin to Baptists and Pentecostalists; in Soviet eyes the three terms are often interchangeable. Some are inoffensive (except in the eyes of the State) and live as the Bible bids, like trusty stewards who expect their Master's return any hour. A few, however, have overfed themselves on the Advent hope until they preach the imminent end of the world with terrifying detail, order their followers to flee the wrath to come by slipping their moorings from anything earthly, or to hasten Christ's coming by provoking the Soviet State to violence and evil until the measure of wickedness be filled to the brim, God's patience is exhausted and He will intervene.

One of the saddest stories of more innocuous delusion typifies the tragedy of those who groan under tyranny. Sometime in the nineteen-fifties a group of sectarians in the Kirghiz Republic in Central Asia, led by one N. P. Goretoi and variously known as Tremblers or Evangelical Christian Pentecostalists, believed that the wrath of the Lord rested on Frunze, the capital, and that the Holy Spirit bade them move. Some left good jobs and pleasant apartments to join the trek with their children and goods, and they came to Barnaul, a city of Western Siberia on the Turk-Sib railway.

In 1957 Goretoi believed that God warned him that Barnaul too was cursed—or so an apostate afterwards affirmed. They wished, said the apostate, to find a town where they would be 'safe from the power of the unjust', and this phrase suggests that all along their desire may have been simply for freedom of worship. They sold up (one version is that they burned their homes) and crossed the length of Siberia to reach Nakhodka, the big port near Vladivostok. The journey was slow and difficult over a distance as far as from London to the Persian Gulf, and they reached Nakhodka destitute but fully expecting (said the apostate) that an ark would come from America, and that on this ark they would sail to a Promised Land.

When the ark did not come one of their preachers, Fyodor Myachin, abandoned the sect and wrote his book *My Break with the Sectarians/Tremblers*, published in Vladivostok in 1958. Others were reported (in 1963) to have been resettled by the Soviet authorities, back at Frunze, where the local Baptists sought to aid them, only to discover that exploded expectations had extinguished faith.

Goretoi certainly did not lose his faith. He, his brother and others united several congregations in Nakhodka area and worked hard until his open ministry came to a summary halt in the dock of the People's Court in Nakhodka in August 1961, accused of the forced conversion of children. His accusers put up his own little girl as witness for the prosecution, but she stood against them with a courage marvellous in a ten-year-old.

'Do you believe in God?' asked the Court Chairman.

'I do.'

'Do you go to the movies?'

'No. They have nothing of interest.'

'How do you know, if you never go?'

She was silent.

'What do you want to become, Liza?'

'We don't think about that. How can I think about any kind of future? Maybe I'll die tomorrow. It's all up to God.'

They said Goretoi had crippled her morally. They said Pioneer scarves had been burned. He had broken families, ruined men physically and psychologically by performance of religious rites.

His supporters testified openly in the witness box against the State's denial of religious freedom, and were rebuked for 'slanderous anti-Soviet statements'. When Goretoi affirmed, as Pentecostalists do, that God was their only leader the court interpreted him as shamelessly wriggling from criminal responsibility by lies.

It was easy to prove that he and many of the others had been in prison during the war, simple to call them wartime fascist traitors.

Goretoi received five years imprisonment, to be followed by 'five years of deportation to remote regions of the country for the crimes he had committed'.

CHAPTER XIX

TIGHTENING THE SCREW

In the autumn of 1963 the Society for Knowledge remarked in its special atheistic journal that 'the Communist Party does not conduct implacable anti-religious propaganda so as to liquidate the believer "as a class" '—as the *Kulaks*, the prosperous peasant farmers, were crushed before the Second World War. By that reckoning the increasing instances of administrative action or discrimination against believers result from nothing more sinister than excessive zeal of local officials.

Such men are undoubtedly in a difficult position. If, in the spirit of Khrushchev's famous Decree of 1954, they scrupulously sit back and wait for religion to be eliminated by education and impersonal propaganda their supporters may rebuke them for liberalism towards religious organizations. If they are active in promoting the Party's intentions but strictly keep the letter of official pronouncements and limit their work on individual believers to persuasion, and as a result have few scalps to display, they risk reprimand for a 'conciliatory attitude'. Should they resolve their dilemma by administrative action, or accept at face value the steady output of hatred, ridicule and contempt and treat believers as criminals or anti-Soviet, and the consequent suffering strengthens religion in the area, the officials may be denounced by the Party for distorting the laws and applying them arbitrarily; or simply for insulting the feelings of believers. A success, of course, brings congratulations whatever their methods.

It would be comforting to ascribe ugly incidents merely to local excess of zeal.

Unhappily, evidence accumulates that around 1959 the highest authorities in the Soviet Government accepted that educational methods were failing to eradicate religion and began to apply sterner measures. Since the Twenty-Second Congress in 1961, with the Third Party Programme's clear call to sweep the land clean of 'survivals' in the next twenty years, the squeeze has been intensified.

In other words, the Soviet Government has abandoned the spirit of Khrushchev's Decree of 1954 and often reverts to the very policy the Decree condemned: administrative interference.

This change of policy was not openly acknowledged for years—not until January 1964.

That month, L. Ilichev, Secretary of the Party's ideological committee, referred to it in an article in *Kommunist*. Having criticized Stalin's wartime concordat, he wrote: 'In the last few years Leninist principles in the field of legislation on religious cults have been restored and the churchmen have been deprived of illegal privileges and concessions.' Ilichev's history is awry, for he ignores the comparative measure of religious freedom in the 'twenties until 1929, and ignores Stalin's post-war repression of religion; but the implication is plain. And this implication is supported by evidence, though this evidence cannot be sifted and presented with clarity and absolute certainty by its very nature: an accidental hint in a Soviet newspaper, a story which spills into a court of law, petitions pushed into the hands of Western tourists as they wander around the markets.

The pressure varies, its direction veers now here, now there. The overall picture, however much it may be denied by Church and Government authorities, is of deliberate, discreet persecution.

One line of attack is the wholesale closing of churches and prayer-houses. This is freely admitted by the State—as proof of the decay of religion, for churches are always said to be closed at the 'unanimous request' of their users or on some equally valid excuse, such as town-planning needs. In this sphere (and in this alone) the facts are less grievous than the aggregate of official claims and news items would suggest: according to these, nearly one-half of all places of worship in the U.S.S.R. have closed since 1959. Very many have closed indeed, but some that were so announced remain open, or congregations have been able to move elsewhere. The Baptist magazine *Bratsky Vestnik* unconsciously reveals this. When the Chairman of the All-Union Council visited Western Siberia at the turn of the year 1962–63 he heard that services at Barnaul were again being held 'after a certain interval',

Slavgorod in the Altai was 'temporarily without a prayer-house' but expected to resume regular services when possible: the Omsk presbyter was hoping to equip a prayer-house and have regular services again. The Novosibirsk Baptists had been obliged to move to a site 'near the River Inn and not far from a wood'.

The fate of the Orthodox Church of the Trinity at Novo-moskovsk in the Ukraine, a beautiful medieval building, was recorded in *Science and Religion* for September 1963. The town soviet late in 1960 formally resolved to confiscate the church, turn it into a museum of local history and rescind the registration of the Orthodox community because 'it had ceased its activities'. By 1963 the injured community, smarting under the injustice and the lie, were more dedicated than ever. And because the town soviet lacked funds to create a museum the medieval architectural gem was serving as a school gymnasium.

At Krasnograd, the next city up the railway, the soviet decreed early in 1962 that the Orthodox church must be demolished for urban development. As, month after month, the ejected believers passed their beloved church, still standing, they grew more and more determined to recover it. They petitioned the Council for Religious Cults, which in this case intervened to restore the church to its people.

The believers at Krasnograd were united. In many places a new regulation has had the effect of splitting a church, for in July 1961 the Patriarchate under direct pressure from the U.S.S.R. Council of Ministers altered the regulation of parishes. The power in finance or other major matters now lies with three officials, churchwarden, assistant churchwarden and treasurer, whose election by the church council requires endorsement by the civil authorities. The civil authorities frequently put in agents or sub-servient churchmen, who can be relied on, if required, to dismiss a priest or arrange that a church be closed 'at the request of believers'. Moreover, the priest is no longer legally a member of his church council or his congregation, merely their employee.

At Postavy in October 1963 the chairman of the church council, A. A. Cherenko, introduced a resolution to reduce the priest's salary. The priest informed the people in his next sermon, as they stood shoulder to shoulder after receiving the Sacrament. Some

156

of them thereupon set upon Cherenko, who fled out of the back
of the church and sought refuge in the caretaker's hut. The lady
caretaker threw him out with the words, 'Beat the Anti-Christ,
but quietly or they'll close the church'!

The church people of Davlekanovo in the western Urals were
at worship one Sunday when Comrade Kharchikov arrived with
a group of thugs and a writ of confiscation; the town soviet
wanted the land for a cinema. The thugs began to carry out
furniture. The believers, says Comrade Kharchikov, 'greatly ob-
structed the closing, and while it was true we succeeded in taking
away the furniture more or less peacefully, the last lorry got away
after certain difficulties. The believer activists, more than sixty of
them, began to shower the District Soviet's Executive Committee
with demands that their church should be opened and what
scurrilities didn't they voice!'

That was in 1960. Late in 1963, despite the urgent need for
another cinema just there, the church still stood, used as a school
gymnasium.

·   ·   ·   ·

For some years priests of the Orthodox Church have been subjected to penal taxation. Their income tax is rumoured to be as
high as eighty per cent; the rumour cannot be substantiated, but
a curious sidelight is thrown by an article in *Sovetskaya Rossiya*,
August 18th 1963 (*If the Swindler Wears a Cassock*), complaining that priests in the Kursk area had not been prosecuted when
they submitted false income returns to evade full weight of the
taxes. Some tolerant revenue officer evidently understood their
difficulties, however reprehensible their action. Financial regulations have also been amended to embarrass churches, and the
faithful complain that the secular authorities 'use the money we
give to the Church, for the building of cinemas and other places
of entertainment'.

A recent twist of another screw caused acute distress among the
Orthodox. In April 1963 instructions were quietly circulated that
clergy must forbid children to receive the Sacrament. For parents
this was a grievous blow, for since Baptism is followed immediately by Chrismation (the equivalent of Confirmation) in Eastern

157

Christianity, infants customarily are given the bread and wine. The bishops passed the order to the clergy, the civil authorities to the churchwardens. It was deeply resented. Churchwardens thereupon asked the local soviets for written instructions; these were refused. Priests said they would tell their congregations, when announcing the change, that it was at the direct request of the soviets. They were told not to, that the matter could rest awhile. In many churches the children continue to come.

At Minsk, however, a local official is said to stand outside the cathedral on the lookout for children. If he sees any inside he has them ejected, well slapped or cuffed as they are thrown out. One boy refused to leave and was afterwards soundly beaten. His mother, a widow having a fine record with the wartime Partisans, a fervent Christian, was accosted (it is said) in her room by another official, who tore down her icons, confiscated the prayer-books she had copied out laboriously by hand and would have arrested her had not her children yelled until the neighbours were aroused. He threatened to have her children removed. 'A new enclosure has been built,' he shouted at her, 'where children of Christian parents will be confined. They will be completely isolated from the pernicious influence of religion.'

Terrified of losing them, the woman fled the town.

Equally grievous stories come from Pochaev (near Ternopol in that part of the Ukraine which was Polish between the wars) with its famous monastery. Reports of persecution at this renowned centre of pilgrimage produced official denials in the early months of 1963, including a statement over the name of the bishop. Notwithstanding, ugly rumours continue. The pilgrims' hostel having been forcibly closed, the inhabitants of the town are forbidden to house pilgrims. On June 6th 1963 an invalid woman lately back from hospital had sheltered six women pilgrims when at about eleven o'clock at night, she, her children and the pilgrims being asleep, someone called Alexandra Golubeva, accompanied by a militiaman, hammered on the door of the house. The militiaman drove the pilgrims into the street, Golubeva seized the children by their legs and, dragging them down from their beds, shouted that parents corrupt their children by taking them to shrines. Their mother had to appear next day at a People's Court, where she was told she ought to be shot and was fined. She implored remission of the fine, for she had no money, but they said her belongings would be sold if she defaulted.

The militia had already expelled most of the monks from the monastery. They had put the aged Abbot in a mental home; believers succeeded in securing his release, but in July 1963 the militia chased him out of a nearby village, arresting those who had travelled to see him. He is, say the faithful, 'a man of great spiritual gifts. We all love and respect him and many people come to visit him and ask for his advice and prayers. He is therefore constantly in trouble.'

These smuggled stories of violence cannot be checked, for no thorough, impartial and unrestricted investigation would be allowed; members of the Executive Committee of the World Council of Churches made such enquiry as they might, when on their way to and from their meeting at Odessa in 1964. (Access to Pochaev is reported restored by direct Moscow order.)

Fully authentic, however, for it appeared in 1962 in the Soviet Press, is the bitter tale of the Baptists at the lignite-mining town of Uzlovaya near Tula. They were unregistered, but lived happily with full knowledge of the local authorities until 1959, when a squad of militant atheists descended on the pits. Not content with lectures, the atheists began a determined canvass of believers' homes, where they were courteously received and their propaganda politely rejected. Such rebuff enraged them. Worship services were interrupted, the canvass continued, week after week, making Christian lives a misery and knocking up a claimed score of twenty apostates; stories in the name of some of them appeared in the newspapers, their voices over the air.

The Baptist presbyter worked in the central electro-mechanical workshop. His dismissal, and direction elsewhere, were engineered, and he had to keep in touch with his flock by letter. After two years of unrestrained badgering the Baptists wrote to the national papers; their letters were not published. They complained to the authorities that constitutional freedom of worship was impeded, and bleakly were reminded of constitutional freedom for anti-religious propaganda. Late in 1961, their private homes invaded almost daily, they resolved on a drastic step. Two girls, twenty-year-old Vera and thirty-year-old Kseniya, volunteered to go on hunger strike.

Believers wrote out letters which they dropped in their neighbours' letter boxes, and posters which they pinned up on walls after dark announcing that Vera and Kseniya would fast to death unless they were all allowed to worship freely.

In the early days of 1962 the two girls went up the little path to Vera's mother's small, neat wooden house and the fast began, supported by visits of the other believers for prayer and praise, who also informed the district prosecutor and begged him to act to save the girls. He did nothing.

After twenty days believers wrote to *Izvestia*. 'We implore you, come, see how things stand, and save them!' Surely nation-wide publicity would bring the end of persecution, the end of the hunger strike.

The *Izvestia* correspondent, G. Volkov, came. He found the girls lying together on a narrow bed, in dressing-gowns and head-scarves. He was impressed that they looked remarkably cheerful despite their ordeal: 'Vera even smiled.' In reply to his questions she said softly, 'We are ready to die for our faith and for justice.'

Her mother said: 'They will fast until the persecution of us by the atheists ceases . . . If the persecutions do not cease let her die.'

The brave girls were forcibly removed to hospital. *Izvestia*, far from sympathizing, called the hunger strike 'blackmail . . . frightful cynicism . . . bestial cruelty', and demanded judgment of the local Baptist leaders 'with all the severity of our laws'.

Eight or nine months later this little community was rumoured to be near desperation.

.   .   .   .

Two cries reached the West in 1963, one a petition signed by many Orthodox, the other a plea from an anonymous Baptist. Neither document was solicited by those who unwittingly became their bearers. Both, unless planted by the secret police, which is almost inconceivable, were incontestably genuine.

The Orthodox petition was hopefully addressed to the Ecumenical Patriarch in Istanbul and the Patriarchs of Jerusalem and

Antioch, 'from the parishioners and pilgrims of the Orthodox Church from the whole of Russia'.

'We kneel in humility before you,' it ran, 'and implore you to come to our aid. Since 1959 the Anti-Christ has redoubled his efforts and has unleased terrible persecution against the Russian Orthodox Church.'

Several pages of incidents follow, leading to the story of Pochaev and its monks: 'Our hearts are bleeding. We cannot bear the sight of these old homeless and persecuted men who have nowhere to go. We implore your Holiness to share our grief with us. We beg you with tears to help ...'

And here, less emotional, without request for help, is the cry from an unknown Baptist.

'Our dear ones in Christ I greet you with the love of the Lord and wish to share our freedom with you.

'1. They have begun to persecute us believers very much. They do not let us have religious gatherings in the regions,[1] they condemn, they confiscate our property, they dismiss us from work, they take away our children.

'2. The Government counts churchworkers as outside the Church.

'3. They don't allow spiritual literature to be written. We cannot even receive from you typewritten documents. They don't let them through.

'4. They jam the religious broadcasts which you broadcast on the radio.

'5. They take away our prayer-houses or pull them down and they send believers into exile.

'6. That's how it is, Ours in Christ.

'They persecute believing youth very, very much and don't admit them to Institutes.'

[1] Presumably referring to the districts outside main cities.

CHAPTER XX

CRIMINALS IN THE DOCK

POCHAEV is a highway of sorrow for more than Orthodox; in July 1962 six Pentecostalists received sentences of three and five years imprisonment and loss of parental rights.

Among their crimes were the distribution of 'reactionary American publications', such as translations of booklets by R. A. Torrey, Oral Roberts and Bible portions issued by the Scripture Gift Mission in London. They had forbidden children to join the Pioneers or go to the cinema. Two children, said a teacher, refused to dance or to sing—probably ditties extolling atheism. Another witness, chairman of a village council, alleged theft of rye and clover: a charge of embezzlement or thieving being frequently produced at these trials.

One of the defendants, called Kuzyk, incriminated himself when the prosecutor asked: 'Would you, if the need arose, defend our fatherland with arms against an enemy?'

Silence.

The question was repeated.

'Since,' replied Kuzyk, 'I consider that man must not kill man, I would not.'

'If your family was attacked by ruffians and killed before your eyes, would you not take up an axe or rifle and kill them?'

Kuzyk glanced across at his little daughter, who in the witness box had bravely stood up for her father and for Christ. Quietly he said: 'I would not kill.'

'Why?'

'Because my conscience would not allow it.'

'But this means you would leave your family at the ruffians' mercy. Why would you do it?'

'Because this is man's destiny which has to be fulfilled.'

'This means you would not defend yourself?'

'No, I would not.'

The Pochaev case was one of a stream in 1962, beginning with a show trial in January at Karaganda, Kazakhstan, when three Pentecostalist leaders were returned to prison, where they had spent much of their adult lives. It is possible they were of an extremist 'Holy Roller' sect, but even when reports are passed over because the defendants may have been deranged or infamous or otherwise conceivably of the lunatic fringe, a bitter list of sectarian trials unfolds for the year 1962. It is not complete, being compiled at random from the Soviet Press of certain areas, and the Press describes only those cases which make graphic warnings or 'exposures'; they are never reported straight as news. Often the only mention is a background article immediately before a trial opens, describing the crimes!

In February, in Istra district near Moscow, five 'chiefs of a society of evangelists' were sentenced to 'banishment with mandatory enlistment in labour', and one older man warned, because they had toured the streets playing thirty-three reels of Christian messages on tape-recorders; a proceeding more courageous than wise in the Moscow environs of 1962. They were arraigned under the decree 'On Intensifying the Struggle Against Persons Who Avoid Socially Useful Labour and Lead an Antisocial Parasitic Way of Life'. Yet these men, who as the prosecution admitted were gentle and humble, had ordinary jobs except for the pensioner, and had merely used spare time.

In May 1962 the presbyter of an unregistered congregation at Shchuchinsk in Northern Kazakhstan was charged with having 'for many years preached sectarian dogmas, spread religious literature and drawn unstable people, particularly children, into the sect'. His sentence was not specified but said to be 'just', the violation of the Criminal Codex that chiefly led him to the dock being probably children's evangelism. In June six Pentecostal preachers were tried at Kharkov. The teachers at the school where the children of one of the younger defendants studied 'laid bare a terrible picture of the sect's pernicious influence', a testimony which, in the context, appears a backhanded tribute to the power of a Christian home. It was claimed that four women, victims of the sect, became ill 'with severe psychological ailments', an equally suggestive testimony which cannot be sifted. Four of the men

163

received sentences of between three years and eighteen months, one recanted and had a suspended sentence, and the chief, Kozelko, was given the stiff penalty of five years 'in a corrective labour colony with an intensified regime'—the hardest of hard labour—together with confiscation of property, and exile from his home area after release.

In September a twenty-three-year-old woman shoemaker at Ashkabad near the Persian border of Turkmenistan, who had stepped into the place of a Pentecostal preacher imprisoned in 1961, was banished for five years by a People's Court, and a seamstress was banished and deprived of her children. In the Ukraine, that month, five years deprivation of freedom with five years subsequent banishment were awarded to each of five Pentecostal preachers at Krivoy Rog, and in Zhdanov on the north coast of the Sea of Azov a Baptist missionary called A. S. Prokofiev got the same sentence. He was a man of courage and resource as well as zeal, for he had flitted back and forth through the Ukraine, Belorussia and the vast spaces of Kazakhstan preaching and distributing typescript sermons, though he well knew the inside of a penal labour camp. He held collective baptisms and, of all daring projects, actually organized a Sunday School in Volnovakha.

Four Pentecostal leaders of the Mary oasis near the Afghan border went to prison for five years in October, having bravely defended their beliefs in court. Early in December a sectarian at Ivanovka, also in Central Asia, had four years.

Trial after trial, sentence after sentence, monotonous to hear, one by one, monotonous as the blows which hammered the nails through the nerves and sinews of the Saviour's hands and feet.

On December 12th 1962 at Semipalatinsk in Kazakhstan an unspecified number of 'illegal' Baptists were condemned. A girl Pioneer alleged behaviour by her aunt and uncle at a New Year's party so peculiar that either she must have been taught what to say by her teacher or it was a prank by hoaxers wishing to discredit the group. The brief incident formed the bulk of the newspaper report, though the trial lasted three days and the real crimes were taking children to secret prayer meetings, not letting them go to the cinema and forbidding them to join the Pioneers—or

164

rather, since despite the voluntary nature of the movement some schools are known to insist on children joining without consent of parents or their own wish, the crime is to remove Pioneer scarves and keep the children from Pioneer functions.

At Alma Ata, one week after the Semipalatinsk trial, the leader of a Baptist splinter group, I. E. Grunvald, received three years and the loss of parental rights over his son Mikhail, who having joined the Baptists would not wear a Pioneer tie. Grunvald had been a drunkard, a wastrel, a blasphemer who had deserted four 'wives' and was converted late in life. He went back to his third wife (presumably the only one to whom he was legally married) and by normal standards would seem to have had an excellent influence on Mikhail. But with excessive convert's zeal Grunvald decided that the flourishing Baptist communities of Alma Ata compromised with the Anti-Christ. He formed his own group, which boycotted elections and People's Courts and undermined 'mass cultural undertakings'. The newspaper *Kazakhstanskaya Pravda* said he was still a drunkard in secret, but such gibes are repeated too frequently to be taken seriously.

.   .   .   .

December 1962 was a bad month. Yet another Christian went to prison for five years on, or shortly before, December 22nd in Smolensk. And it was said at another trial in Belorussia that a five-year-old boy had hanged himself as the result of being left in care of his zealous Baptist granny ! A suspiciously similar case was reported a month later, on January 24th 1963 at the opposite end of the U.S.S.R., when a twelve-year-old boy at a place on the Ussuri river in the Soviet Far East was said to have committed suicide through the 'venom of Christian fanaticism' of his granny. Her relative, a Baptist preacher, was banished to a designated area.

In 1963 fewer cases were reported, though as many may have occurred.

A Baptist preacher called Ivanenko was arrested while with the recognized and flourishing Baptist church at Tashkent, where he had been living two or three years. At his trial in March 1963 the authorities claimed he was really someone else, a wartime traitor;

that he had changed his name and become a leading Baptist, had married, failed to win his wife to the faith and deserted her and their children. His major crime seems to have been that at Moscow in 1958 he provided an American tourist with 'slanderous "information" about the position of believers in the U.S.S.R. and gave him some sectarian twaddle he had hashed up for use in the programmes of the "Voice of America".' His sentence was not reported.

A tragic case emerged in May, of men and women near Brest (Brest-Litovsk) who had gone to great lengths for their faith.

Back in 1961 three hundred Baptists had declined to merge with an officially recognized community in a village near by and thus subordinate themselves to the All-Union Council. They were ordered to destroy their building and refused; the town soviet forcibly pulled it down by hitching a rope and tractor to each end. The Baptists went to ground. They met in little groups in each other's houses, switching from suburb to suburb to fox the authorities. Their leader who (if the customary allegations have substance in this case) had been an active Ukrainian nationalist after the Soviet invasion of 1939, organized activities on an almost military scale. The members distributed literature, recorded overseas Gospel broadcasts and circulated the tapes, went on missionary journeys to distant parts. In Brest they had secret Sunday Schools, young people's Bible circles, a choir and a string orchestra.

A happy, pulsating example of vigorous Christian endeavour— which landed four leaders in the dock of a criminal court on May 13th 1963. Sentences have never been reported.

·   ·   ·   ·

The bitter record continues. Five Seventh Day Adventists found themselves before the court in Irkutsk, Siberia, in June, but no word has been heard of the upshot.

In November 1963 a savage sentence was meted out to a Baptist youth, with lesser sentences on his mother and two other women, after a three-day trial at Namangan in the Fergana Valley, 120 miles east of Tashkent. Granny Shevchuk had become a Baptist 'because God drew me into the community. He healed me from a very serious illness.'

The trial judge demanded:

'Did you at this time turn to the doctors?'

'Yes, I turned to the doctors. But it is God, you know, who heals the sick through people.'

Granny Shevchuk was no starry-eyed faith-quack, but a simple Christian who had found God at a time of physical affliction and in gratitude served Him with all her heart. She sought out the little Baptist church at Namangan, which was unregistered and thus illegal; the atheists were strong, the Christians met secretly. She became a deeply loved leader. Metropolitan Nicholas once said, 'Every old woman among the Baptists is a missionary,' and Granny Shevchuk was no exception. Sometimes she would hear of a sick woman among unbelieving neighbours and with other Baptists go 'and ask God to heal her'.

'Well, and did He heal her?' questioned the judge.

'Yes, He did.'

'And did they send for the doctor?'

'Yes they sent for him.' The court laughed, thought it a great joke. Mrs. Shevchuk pitied their ignorance.

She had sought to win her sick brother and his wife. They rebuffed her, but two other women, Mrs. Tkachenko and Mrs. Vekazina, became 'as great fanatics' as Mrs. Shevchuk. She taught her young granddaughter Baptist hymns and, because there was acute shortage of Bibles in the community, and her granny was probably semi-illiterate, little Lyuba copied out passages from their aged Old Testament, printed before the Revolution, to pass round to others, while someone with a New Testament did likewise. That Lyuba learned a true love of the Saviour is evident from the court's comments on the 'pernicious effect on the girl and on the formation of her character and world outlook' of her granny's 'criminal activities'.

Granny was sent to prison for two years. Her friends and converts, Taisiya Tkachenko, who told fellow toilers at the textile factory, 'You are going along the wrong road, you are sheep which have strayed,' and Ekaterina Vekazina, who boldly affirmed before the court, 'We wished to bring all the world into our sect,' also received two years.

The savage sentence on that November day of 1963, just one

week before the assassination of President Kennedy, was reserved for Mrs. Vekazina's boy, Georgi Vekazin.

He was described as an 'adolescent youth', which suggests an age not much more than twenty, yet he had already served in a labour colony, having been sentenced for 'stealing'; probably he had accepted money for the spread of the Gospel. Rough treatment in the labour camp had not shattered Georgi's faith. He came home in February 1963 with calloused hands and uncowed spirit, and at once became a secret evangelist. He grew friendly with the girl next door, aged fourteen. She was often in the Vekazin home, and it would seem she was about to become a Christian when her parents stepped in: presumably they shared the local antagonism for those who 'were trying to tear people away from a seething life and from participation in the building of Communism.'

They said he raped her.

Georgi is now in prison for eight years.

The year 1964 carries forward the harsh tally of trials. In February two young men of Tashkent, a foreman-painter and a storeman, and the father-in-law of one of them, all members of an independent Baptist group, received sentences (unspecified) for circulating typewritten Christian literature and holding prayer-meetings; even the court admitted that their characters were exemplary. In March, near Yekabpils in Latvia, a Pentecostalist couple called Pilat were sent to prison, the wife for four years, the husband for three. They had already been deprived of their children, their crime being the bringing them up to Christian faith. During the same month three more members of the much persecuted group of Baptists in Brest received prison sentences of eight, five and three years. It was said they were swindlers and speculators but as their defence was suppressed in the Press, the truth cannot be known.

In May 1964 came the report of three young Baptists of Kulunda in the Altai Territory who received sentences of five and three years for recruiting adolescents to their independent group, preaching non-co-operation with the State, and holding a Bible school and secret prayer-meetings.

WHEN KHRUSHCHEV STUDIES

MR. KHRUSHCHEV has always been vocal about religion, but his actions belie his words.

In 1956, two years after his Decree, he told some Indonesians: 'We respect every group which declares its belief in any religion whatsoever, although we ourselves do not believe in God. Now that the Soviet regime rests on a secure foundation, the Communist Party and the Government will show greater indulgence towards church authorities.' In 1959 he answered the leader of a delegation from India: 'From your speech one might draw the conclusion that as an atheist I don't like religious people. But this idea is wrong. You are right in saying that I am not a religious man, whereas you believe in religion. But that should not lead anyone to conclude that there must be any hostility or animosity between us . . . As atheists we do not allow ourselves to feel any antagonism towards religious-thinking people. We have never promoted animosity between people for religious reasons, nor do we intend to do so in future. We treat religious people not only with tolerance but with respect.' These words, spoken at the very time when pressure was hardening, might have seemed utterly cynical had he not added: 'We only attack if religion is exploited in order to harm human beings. Then we really get active.'

He and his friends can twist all religion in Russia to that specification.

Khrushchev would seem divided in his own mind. In Iowa during his American tour he actually stated, 'If you look into our political philosophy you will see we have a lot of Christian precepts, such as loving your neighbour'; thus implicitly denying that Christian teaching is a fraud derived from a fiction. Had a Party official uttered such words publicly in the U.S.S.R., he would have been denounced. Walter Kolarz in a broadcast once queried whether 'Khrushchev has really fully solved the problem of religion for himself personally'.

Perhaps one day the thought will strike him that since he despises and abhors an unplanned society, and glories in the role of Chief Planner, he is somewhat illogical to harry and frustrate those who acknowledge the existence of a Planner in the Universe, who believe that nature and man are not the consequence of chance developed by chaos. Perhaps he will order an objective survey of the character and activity of the religious minority; a survey not conducted according to Party preconception but honest, fair and fearless, and then will study the Christian religion, its history and literature and worship, as it is and has been, not as the Party line distorts and misinterprets.

And despite all that is unChrist-like in Christianity, he will awake to awareness that a small group of strident and atheist fanatics are using the Communist Party and the Soviet Government to impose on a mighty nation their own bleak, narrow ideas based on 'Fundamental Bases' so inadequate, ill-formed and childish that were the effects less tragic they would be the laughing-stock of philosophers (Christian or no) outside Eastern Europe; ideas that do not dare challenge an uncrippled opposition, yet barely make headway with all the advantage behind them of a strong favourable wind of partisan legislation.

Khrushchev has a sense of humour. Let him tell the atheists that henceforth they meet opponents in fair fight, and see if they can win.

Let him tell them the Russian people are children no longer, but mature enough to hear all sides of the great arguments that concern man's spirit and its destiny, and to choose whom they will serve.

.   .   .   .

There is no sign, no hint of dawn in the night that lies around the believers of Soviet Russia.

Yet the Party line by which Soviet Russia decides her policy has changed or developed in other spheres, could change in this.

.   .   .   .

The Cuban Crisis, and America's courageous stand, made Khrushchev abandon threat of nuclear war as an instrument of diplomacy, thus lifting a shadow from all the peoples of the world.

Some two months later the Thirty Two Siberians broke into the light of the world's knowledge and disappeared back into the darkness.

Is it possible—this is audacious, perhaps far-fetched—that in long perspective the brave action of the Thirty Two will be found to have led, slowly yet ultimately, to the lifting of the shadow of religious persecution from the people of Khrushchev's own land?—by forcing the world's attention; causing the world to seek the facts of the whole situation, and to press those facts on Khrushchev until in his desire for the happiness of his people he realigns the Party.

Who, then, were the Thirty Two Siberians?

CHAPTER XXI

THE FLIGHT OF THE THIRTY TWO

THE story of the Thirty Two began when a young man of about thirty, Grigory Vashchenko, and his wife, settled at the coal-mining village of Rakitov Klyuch near Chernogorsk in the early nineteen-fifties. Chernogorsk, which means 'Black Mountain', is the centre of a small coalfield on the lower slopes of the Abakan mountains in the western borders of Eastern Siberia.

It is not known whence Vashchenko came or why.[1] He may have been deported from the Ukraine, or been born somewhere in Siberia. Perhaps he was searching for his father, who is known to have been released from a penal camp, or came to Chernogorsk as the result of a labour directive. He may have been just a wandering missionary. By trade a jobbing builder, he was a man of strong, simple Christian faith. The older Vashchenko, twice imprisoned, had passed his fervour to his sons, for Grigory was joined at Rakitov Klyuch by his younger brothers, Khariton, who was a surgeon's assistant, Peter, and Pavel, and all were believers.

Chernogorsk, on a short spur of railway near the end of the branch line which runs more than 200 miles to join the Trans Siberian at Achinsk, has a long tradition of evangelical Christianity. In the mountains and along the nearby Yenisei river to the east little groups had sprung up among the exiles in Tsarist times, and one of Baedeker's party had come among them during the Anglo-German evangelist's journey across Siberia visiting the

[1] Some of the details in the story of the Thirty Two are inevitably conjectural, based on reasonable deductions from available clues. The account put out, in English for foreign consumption, by the Soviet Agency *Novosti*, on January 9th 1963, six days after the incident at the American Embassy, can hardly be relied on, since it followed the Party propaganda line about sectarians with suspicious exactness, even to hackneyed phrases ('clandestine fanatics', 'savage rites', etc.) and the usual stories of embezzlement, cruelty, etc. It was also callously flippant. Some of its major points were directly contradictory to firm evidence gathered in other ways.

prisons. When Grigory began to preach, therefore, in the last years of Stalin, his words caught at the hearts of miners and their wives as they crowded into the Vashchenko home. The old songs, *I want to love more strongly, Forward after Him,* and twenty or thirty others were heard again, wafted on the freezing wind from behind closed and curtained windows in winter, or from woods beyond the slag heaps in the hot Siberian summer.

Grigory and his brothers preached a robust gospel of a basically biblical mould: there seem to have been no perversions or diseased twists. It was an uncompromising gospel, shot through with the love of God yet stern in refusal to compromise with the Anti-Christ. It was joyous, uninhibited: whatever the Communists said afterwards, the Vashchenkos' were happy homes. These Christians were ruggedly independent too: they reckoned each other equal before God, nor should they be subservient to any Baptist Council 2,000 miles away in Moscow, nor to a senior presbyter in Novosibirsk which, more than 400 miles distant by rail, seemed to men of Chernogorsk almost in another country.

The flame of passionate preaching rose higher. These men of God made converts; the revival of faith passed from one village to another among Russian settlers and the native Khakassy. The Anti-Christ was roused. The Vashchenkos were ordered to stop 'conducting sectarian propaganda and recruiting gullible people'; thenceforth the groups in the villages met secretly, but they sang as before. By now, in the late 'fifties, they numbered several hundred.

The serious clash came when some of the sect withdrew children from school. Valya Vashchenko, eldest daughter of Khariton, had already reached the fifth grade and was rising twelve when she came home one day (or so it would seem) reporting that a new teacher had arrived. Now they were being forced to learn and repeat blasphemies about God and Christ and told the Bible was a tissue of fairy tales; previously, religion and anti-religion had been ignored. Valya was upset. Far from being a cowering child whipped by her parents into aping Christian belief, she was a militant Christian.

Disgust at blasphemies she was told to repeat, and refused to repeat, made Valya the more determined that neither she nor her younger sister Tanya, and little brother, Peter, who both adored her and looked to her for leadership, should deny Christ. She grew thoroughly unhappy. Mr. and Mrs. Khariton Vashchenko took the extreme—and unlawful—step of withdrawing their children.

The revolt spread. Thirty children of Chernogorsk district were withdrawn from schools. The teachers were indignant. Local Party officials took notice and organized a 'public drive'. The sectarians of each village were ordered to attend a public meeting at which miners, teachers and deputies of the Chernogorsk soviet denounced them for 'savage violations of human rights'. The usual accusations were hurled at them: that they beat their children, refused to let them play, were driving them mad; Alexei Kudashkin, a veteran of Stalin's penal camps, was alleged to have tied his eighteen- or twenty-year-old son to a bed with rope and electric wire, and to have forced him to fast and pray for six weeks, mentally crippling him for life.

In consequence of the public drive a People's Court, late in 1961 or early in 1962, sentenced the Khariton Vashchenkos and others to loss of parental rights. The children would be sent to one of the new boarding-schools or internats. It was said by the *Novosti* Agency that Grigory Vashchenko, founder of the sect, and one of the other leaders called Miller, were given terms of imprisonment; but either these were unusually brief or the report was in error, for had they received suspended sentences they would not have remained in possession of their internal passports which enabled them to travel.

The news that Valya, her sister, and little Peter, too, were to be removed to an internat caused agony in the Vashchenko home. For the first time they talked of emigration.

Until then the Vashchenkos had seen themselves as missionaries to their own people, called upon to withstand the Anti-Christ and fight him on his own ground by prayer and preaching. The Anti-Christ had now cut at the tenderest spot—the happiness of the Christians' children. As the members of the sect wept and prayed in each other's homes, the desire to continue worshipping according to conscience, and to bring up their children in the fear of the Lord, over-rode the compulsion to win Him more disciples. Most of the sect were in their prime: life stretched ahead and they

174

desired to be free. The laceration of family ties, the tearing of mother from daughter, father from son, was a grief hardly to be borne: it drove right into the devotion to their children which is so marked among Russians. For the sectarians it had the added horror that their children might lose faith, be unable, as they grew, to resist the weight of atheist persuasion. Grigory and his wife shared his brother's grief and saw the day coming when their own, younger family would be cut off too.

In their simplicity none of them seem to have understood how emigration was regarded by the Soviet Government.

. . . .

Valya, aged twelve, Tanya aged eight, and Peter, who was only seven, were taken to an internat at Zaozernyy, beyond the provincial capital, Krasnoyarsk; 250 miles by river steamer and rail from home. They had never been away before.

Though legally removed from parental jurisdiction, the children could not be prevented from slipping letters in the town post box. The Vashchenkos were heart-broken to read Tanya's fate: 'I cry at night,' she wrote. 'The boys beat me. But don't worry, Papa and Mama—God still keeps us. Valya and I cry because they don't let us go home. Mamochka, come!' Mamochka did come—travelled 250 miles to come, and was refused a sight of her children.

'MAMA, THE BOYS HERE BEAT ME,' spelled out little Peter in capital letters, 'BUT I BEAR EVERYTHING. MAMA, I BEG THEM TO LET ME GO HOME, BUT THEY WON'T LET ME.'[1]

The weary weeks of 1962 in that Siberian school with its portraits of a benevolent Lenin, its drill and lessons and games, wore on. Valya bravely attempted to say grace before meals, though the other girls stood around and stopped her. 'I tell them I won't eat until I ask God's blessing.' They teased and yelled 'Pray-baby! Pray-baby!' When she felt sad and bitter she would creep away to write to her parents, or, tactless but valiant, sing psalms

[1] The originals of these and other letters from the children were left at the American Embassy. Translations were published in part in *Newsweek*, January 28th 1963. For the full texts I am indebted to the courtesy of *Newsweek*.

with Tanya and Peter. This infuriated the School Director. 'Mamochka,' wrote Valya, 'The Director shouts at us—and that is good. The deeper the grief, the closer we are to God. With the help of God I will believe in Him. I will not study in a godless school. Don't cry Mamochka, but pray for us, pray that we should stand firm.'

To her father she wrote: 'If they won't let us emigrate, then let them kill us. I'm tired of living in these conditions.'

The Director decided that Valya should become a Pioneer. She refused, but refusal was not hers to make, for legally the Director stood *in loco parentis*, though he frustrated the spirit of a voluntary movement; nor should unsuitable candidates be admitted. Enrolment day came. The whole school paraded. The selected candidates stood in a group before a table on which were laid Pioneer three-pointed red scarves. One by one they stepped forward to take the oath and don a scarf.

'Valya Vashchenko,' called the Director.

She stepped forward, head held high.

'Take the oath, Valya!'

Valya's mouth stayed shut tight.

'Valya! say the oath, Valya! . . . Very well, I will read it in your name.' He pointed to two other girls. 'You will place the scarf on Valya's neck as I read.'

He began: 'I, a young Pioneer of the U.S.S.R., before my comrades—young patriots deciding the question of my admission into the organization—promise that I shall stand firmly for the cause of Lenin and for the victory of Communism. I promise . . .'

His words were drowned as Valya burst out in prayer to God and began to sing a hymn at the top of her voice:

'We will stand firm for the Gospel faith, for Christ,
Following His example, forward all, forward after Him.'

After this incident Valya sat down and composed a letter to Prime Minister Khrushchev: 'I have had enough of being unhappy,' she wrote. 'I don't want to live any more in the Soviet Union. Either kill me or let me go to Israel. Of course in the Soviet Union there is no compulsion. Why, then, did the school force me to take the Pioneer's oath? But I stood and sang psalms

176

while they forced me to put on the uniform. I tell you I won't study in a godless school.'

.　　　.　　　.　　　.

Valya sent the letter to her parents with a request that they forward it to Mr. Khrushchev. When they received it emigration was discussed seriously at Chernogorsk.

The whole approach was pathetically muddled and naïve. The sect leaders had heard of the State of Israel, but confused it with the Biblical Zion; they knew nothing of a Jewish national home. They do not seem, either, to have imagined Israel as a mythical fairyland, but as a place across the sea where the ransomed of the Lord had returned, a Christian land where all might worship God freely and happily. They had heard of America: some of their relatives would have emigrated in Tsarist times. It is possible too that they identified America with Israel or, influenced by the stream of anti-American propaganda, supposed the chief opponent of the Anti-Christ must be the Land of Christ, of Zion. They knew that America allowed freedom of worship.

They did not contemplate illegal exit from the U.S.S.R. They wished to emigrate. They had forwarded Valya's letter to Mr. Khrushchev, so he, they presumed, already knew about it personally and was helping them.

They little realized that emigration from the U.S.S.R. is a concession granted rarely, with almost infinite delay, on highly compassionate grounds, such as a foreign spouse or a parent living abroad—or to those emigrating to serve the interests of the Soviet State. Request for a group exit visa would be almost a joke to the Kremlin. No *Mayflower* had ever sailed from Soviet Russia.

In secret meetings in the Chernogorsk villages during the middle months of 1962 family after family, as they prayed, grew certain that God was leading them on the path to emigration, that He had a definite purpose in thrusting them forward. Sad as they would be to leave home, they looked on the distant prospect with delight.

They decided that a small number should go ahead, secure permission, settle down in Israel (or America-Zion) and send for the rest to follow, nearly 500 in all. When Chernogorsk was baking in the heat of a Siberian summer one man, as scout for the group, with funds scraped together by the others, made the long journey by the Trans-Siberian to Moscow and back. Whether he handed in the petition requesting permission to leave the country, or whether it went by post is not clear. The possibility had crossed their minds that permission would not be granted without a struggle, and he explored alternative means of persuading Mr. Khrushchev.

The autumn months passed with no word from Mr. Khrushchev or his officials.

The Chernogorsk Christians began to fear that permission might not be forthcoming without outside help. Each village congregation began to compose a petition to the Americans.

·　　　·　　　·　　　·

In November or early December shattering news reached the sect. More of their children were to be removed to internats on January 1st 1963. The parents were appalled. Time now was of the essence, and they resolved that the advance party, including the children whom the State was about to steal, should leave Chernogorsk before the end of December. Travelling the Trans-Siberian in mid-winter was not their choice. The alternative would be worse.

A further difficulty now loomed. Mr. Khrushchev's permission not having been received, they might have to see him, and leave the country before the children already in internats, including Valya, Tanya and little Peter, could be released to rejoin them. They therefore prepared a letter to U Thant asking for United Nations intervention. The one brighter gleam was a rumour that some of their children had been transferred to an internat at Moscow. They would be able to pick them up.

On or about December 29th six men of varying ages, twelve women and fourteen children slipped down quietly in two or three inconspicuous groups from their different villages to Chernogorsk station. Grigory Vashchenko was their leader. With him were Peter and Augustina Vashchenko and their children Lida, Lyuba and Nadya. The Khariton Vashchenkos were there, and the youngest brother, Pavel, or Miller. Alexei Kudashkin was the oldest of the six men, thirty-two-year-old Mikhail Morgachev the youngest.[1] All were dressed in typical peasant winter clothing: thick quilted or skin coats, knee-length felt boots, skin caps. The women wore cotton dresses under their heavy topcoats.

They took tickets to Achinsk, the junction for the Trans-Siberian. As they mingled with the other travellers on the hard-packed snow of the open platform waiting for the train, and their breath rose like steam in the sharp frost, no one else took the slightest notice. They had their (internal) passports; the journey was legal.

At Achinsk, where they were not known and their movements would not be easily traced, they booked for Moscow and climbed on to the long green coaches of the Trans-Siberian Express, to endure the journey of two days and nights sitting up on the crowded benches of a lower-class carriage.

New Year's Day, 1963, came while the train chugged noisily across the almost imperceptible watershed of the wooded Urals. Unless the hue and cry was raised in Chernogorsk when the children could not be found, and the local authority with most unusual speed traced them half over Russia before they had seen Mr. Khrushchev and explained all, they were safe.

[1] The names were released by the *Novosti* Agency.

CHAPTER XXII

THE CRY OF THE THIRTY TWO

THE Thirty Two seem to have reached Moscow on January 2nd 1963. They shuffled down the stairs at the Kurksky terminus and round into the enormous high-ceilinged waiting-room with its air of a decayed ballroom.

The tiring journey had tried the children badly. Two had bad colds, others were listless with excessive fatigue. The party had nowhere to go, had eaten little, money was short; they did not think the Chernogorsk militia would catch up with their movements, but time obviously was running out. The sooner they left Russia, the better.

Grigory Vashchenko settled them on the benches of the waiting-room, walked into the beaten snow of the wide forecourt, past the Metro to the bus- and trolley-bus-stop on the wide main street. It is not known to which Ministry he went to ask about their petition and arrange to see Mr. Khrushchev, but there can be little doubt that he was kept all day along with a score of other callers, and that even if he spoke to a junior clerk, he had not seen any person of the slightest authority before work ended and suppliants were turned into the street.

The slow processes of Soviet bureaucracy had barely yet had time to notice his existence, but to Grigory the answer was a decided negative: Mr. Khrushchev did not wish to see him. The original request for permission to emigrate had been sent months earlier. By now, Valya's letter would have been read and re-read by the Prime Minister, and the Prime Minister did not care.

Grigory would have called back the next day had not the health of the children deteriorated during the long night of January 2nd, which they spent in the waiting-room. The Thirty Two might have been any group of families such as reached Moscow from the Ukraine or the Baltic or the north and spent a night at the station before boarding a train for Siberia or the Far East.

In the earlier hours of January 3rd the leaders of the Thirty Two huddled together and made up their minds. Hungry, cold and weary, they would hesitate no longer. While it was still dark the Siberians picked up their bundles and the younger children in their tight-bound 'cocoons' and trudged into the bitter cold. They began to walk westwards along the street which, as it circled round past the Sklifosovsky Institute and the Tchaikovsky Concert Hall, would at long last become Tchaikovsky Street and take them direct to the American Embassy.

The day grew light. Snow began to fall. A small child, deep in its 'cocoon' of skins, whimpered. Its father changed the burden from one arm to another, but his heart was light. They had been ambling along at the pace of the slowest for an hour and a half at the least, and soon would reach the gate, and a moment or two later gain Christian ground. *'Slava Bogu!'* murmured Grigory, 'Glory be to God!'

'Slava Bogu,' the others echoed.

·   ·   ·   ·

With a shout and a cry they were through the militiamen, under the archway and into the American Embassy at about 9.15 a.m. on January 3rd 1963 as the staff were beginning the day's work.

'Save us and help us!' cried the Siberians.

Old Gaffer Kudashkin, in frayed brown overcoat with tears streaming down his rugged face, shouted to the astonished Americans, 'There is no place for us in the Soviet Union. We demand of those who believe in Christ and God—help us! This is,' he added in his muddled way, 'the Embassy of Israel, isn't it?'

When the confusion and uproar subsided the Thirty Two were shepherded into the small courtyard used as a car park, where in summer Embassy children play cowboys and Indians, at the back of the main building. Harrassed officials not unnaturally were still barely aware what these strange invaders wanted, and whether they should summarily be thrust into the street. When it became obvious they were in distress, no American would have turned

181

them out before discovering the cause. After a little delay Grigory Vashchenko was taken to talk with a senior officer, a fluent linguist. The rest were led into the hall outside the community room, and a meal of coffee, bacon and eggs prepared.

Grigory told the officer they wished to go to Israel, 'where God's law is taught, not persecuted'. He begged for shelter until they could leave the country, for help in securing passages. He told how they had sought to live for God and bring up their children to love Him, that the Soviet authorities refused to allow them to do so. He showed the children's letters from the internat, spoke of Valya's forced Pioneer oath, described the 'public drive' against the Christians, the ignoring of their petition and the letter to Mr. Khrushchev. He mentioned the children believed to be in Moscow over 2,000 miles from home; could the Embassy please reunite them before sending the whole group to Israel? Grigory took a gulp at the cup of coffee which had stood untouched by his chair.

The officer spoke. His tone was kind and gentle. Grigory was appalled and incredulous to hear that the whole request was impossible. By international usage Soviet citizens must have Soviet permission to emigrate. The Embassy could not act on its own.

Grigory refused to believe it. The mighty Christian nation surely could do what it liked now the Siberians were on American soil. He began to recapitulate their miseries.

Grigory Vashchenko's passionate faith in God (and in the Americans), his urgency, the crystal sincerity of his plea that they must be allowed to worship and love God freely, made the interview an agony. The officer would have done anything to help, but was bound. The Siberians were not in imminent danger of their lives, the sole ground on which asylum could be granted; they had not asked asylum, only for help in emigrating and shelter until they could go.

Another officer meanwhile had consulted the Ambassador and then telephoned the Soviet Ministry of Foreign Affairs.

The Siberians other than Vashchenko were eating their meal, content that the battle was over, that soon they would be on their way to Israel.

Arguing, Grigory Vashchenko would not be convinced. He

was sure the hand of God had led them to Moscow; he could not see that in leading them God had a higher and wider purpose than their safety or freedom, that theirs must be still the way of the cross.

. . . .

The Embassy officer took Vashchenko along to rejoin the others. The officer told them, kindly but firmly, that their request could not be granted and that officials of their own country were coming to take them from the Embassy.

The Siberians received the news with stark, numbing disbelief.

At 11 a.m. a highly embarrassed official of the Protocol Division of the Soviet Foreign Office, Kolokolov, and the militia commander of the Embassy guard, Shpakov, arrived at the Embassy. They were taken to the officer who had seen Vashchenko.

Kolokolov said the American: 'I wish to apologize to the Embassy for this incident, on behalf of the Foreign Office and the Soviet Government. We have no idea why the American Embassy was chosen for this demonstration. As is well known, religious freedom is guaranteed in the Soviet Union. There are no reprisals against parents who do not wish their children to join the Pioneers. I can assure you that these people will be treated with utmost consideration.'

To this speech the Embassy officer replied formally that the United States had no wish to be involved in complaints of Soviet citizens against conditions in the U.S.S.R.; the American Embassy was chosen by them because of the well-known American belief in religious freedom.

He then said: 'You may have difficulties in persuading them to leave without convincing assurances that there will be no reprisals. An assurance that the group could visit some of the children alleged to be in Moscow would go far towards facilitating their departure. Medical attention for the sick and a heated bus would also be desirable.' He added that the Embassy would be most interested to learn the fate of the refugees and how their case finally was settled by the Soviet authorities.

The officer would have known as he spoke how forlorn was this last request. No news ever reached the Embassy; nothing but the scurrilous, unfeeling *Novosti* handout with its claim that the group were attempting to 'evade responsibility for their evil deeds' and were being returned to Siberia, where 'we hope the public of Chernogorsk will help these "Christians" to regain human dignity'—an ominous statement in the context of Communist use of the phrase 'human dignity'. And six weeks later, on February 14th, an English-language broadcast from Moscow for Eastern North America answered a Texan listener's letter: 'They certainly were not punished. In comfortable sleeping cars they returned to their homes in Siberia.' The rest of the brief broadcast attacked the 'fanatical sect that knew absolutely no bounds', repeated some of the *Novosti* allegations and ended: 'When people protested against the actions of this fanatic sect, they tried to pretend that the Soviet Government was attempting to deprive them of their freedom of religion, which is a lot of nonsense, you'll agree, because this fanaticism has absolutely nothing in common with religion.'

Valya, Tanya and little Peter would *not* have agreed.

After that, silence.

.   .   .   .

The Embassy officer, having made his request for further information, took Kolokolov and Captain Shpakov to the community room at about 11.30 to confront the Siberians.

The atmosphere in the Embassy was electric. Everyone knew what had happened and was about to happen. The Western correspondents in Moscow had gathered in the courtyard, stamping their feet against the bitter cold.

Captain Shpakov addressed the Siberians. His words were honeyed. He said they would be given rooms at a hotel near a railway terminus (nothing was afterwards known of them at the hotel he named). They would get medical attention (this at least seems to have been provided) and sent home.

'We do not want to go home,' replied Grigory on behalf of the others. 'We want to go to Israel. We want to worship God freely. We want our children.'

'I assure you, citizens, you will be given fullest opportunity to present individual complaints and requests for exit visas. They will be thoroughly investigated.'

'We don't believe you. Our requests have been ignored. You'll punish us.'

'I assure you, you have committed no crime in entering the Embassy. Reprisals will not be taken against you.'

'We don't believe you!' replied Grigory.

'We don't believe you,' echoed old Alexei Kudashkin. 'There is no place for us in the Soviet Union. Let us go to Israel.' He turned to the Embassy officer. 'Comrade American, let us go. Please let us go to Israel! They will shoot us here.'

'Yes, they will arrest us,' said another. 'Comrade American, if you believe in Christ and in God, help us!'

The American explained again that there was no way by which the Embassy could ship them out of Soviet territory without Soviet permission.

The minutes ticked by. Repeated promises by Shpakov and Kolokolov made no headway. Some of the women bowed their heads in prayer. Kudashkin wept. Grigory Vashchenko argued. To the Americans in the room it was as if a crucifixion in all its horror and brutality was being prepared. They knew there could be one end only to the colloquy: the Siberians must leave. The Americans found it difficult to trust Soviet assurances. And however the Soviet news-handout might present the story later, the Americans had not the slightest doubt that the Siberians were genuine believers in acute distress. Jesus Christ was being openly displayed upon His cross before their eyes.

At about 12.30 Grigory Vashchenko agreed to go.

Whether he had seen now that theirs must be the way of the cross, that they were being called to suffer shame for His name and like Peter of old should rejoice; that God's purpose must be not their rescue but the revealing to the Christian world of the agony of Russian believers—or whether he had merely recognized the futility of remaining in the Embassy, Grigory led his people to the door.

In the archway a Soviet bus was standing, with high wooden panels beside its door blocking the correspondents' view; at their protest they were taken down, but Kolokolov demanded that no photographs be taken, and the Embassy concurred: one correspondent who attempted to take one later outside the Embassy when the bus emerged had his arm thrust up by a plain-clothes militiaman. Nor were interviews allowed.

Some of the Siberians climbed into the bus.

The others jibbed. The colloquy was resumed. For a half-hour more, while the snow fell again, officials and Siberians argued.

Gaffer Alexei turned to the newsmen and shouted: 'There is no place for believers in the Soviet Union! We know they will shoot us sooner or later.'

Several of the Siberians, men and women, wept openly.

Another turned to the newsmen and American onlookers and again came the cry: 'Those who believe in God and Christ help us. We ask it. We ask that those who believe in God and Christ help us.'

These words wrung the hearts of newsmen hardened by witnessing violence and sorrow all over the world. The words echoed round, and still echo. 'We ask it. Help us,' help not only the Thirty Two but the thousands upon thousands of nameless believers across one-sixth of the world's surface, including that great majority who would never seek to emigrate but, in the Soviet environment where God has placed them, live quietly as loyal citizens, bravely as unashamed Christians—the people about whom this book has been written . . .

Most of the Siberians, sadness on their faces, at length boarded the bus. A few wandered off across the courtyard, the spectators making way, respectfully, sympathetically, doubtful what they intended to do.

As the doors closed, and the bus started up, this little party walked slowly in physical weariness and in sorrow towards the south gate, where they stood uncertainly in the archway. Did a half-hope of escape cross their minds? Did they look for the Lord to take them by a miracle? Did they seek just to gather their thoughts, to face the way of the cross?

The vehicle turned right into the traffic and drew up by the south entrance near the bus-stop. The doors were opened again.

Without protest the last of the Thirty Two let themselves be locked inside.

REFERENCES AND SOURCES

N.i.R.=*Nauka i Religiya*

V.P.P.S.=*V. Pomoshch Politicheskomu Samoobrazovaniyu*

PART ONE

REFERENCES WHERE NOT MENTIONED IN THE TEXT

Chapter I

Soviet theory of freedom of conscience: *N.i.R.*, 1960, Nos. 5, 12; 1961, No. 4; *Sovetskoe Gosudarstvo i Pravo*, 1959, No. 3

Chapter II

Commentary on Third Party Programme: *N.i.R.*, 1961, No. 3
Lenin on Religion: *Works*, 10, pp. 65–6

Chapter III

On Billy Graham: *N.i.R.*, 1961, No. 9

Chapter IV

Gaevskaya's activities: *V.P.P.S.*, 1962, No. 4
Izvestia's list of atheist activities: November 1st 1963
The anti-religious snoopers: *N.i.R.*, 1963, No. 7
Baturin's pamphlet: published by Gospolitizdat, 1962
The lecturer who refused to go: *Izvestia*, November 1st 1963

Chapter V

On atheist films, etc.: *N.i.R.*, 1961, No. 5; 1963, No. 3
Foreign view of Anti-God Museum: *God and the Soviets*, by Marcus Bach, 1958, p. 22
The Lithuanian newspaper: see *Sovetskaya Litva*, July 11th 1963

Interlude

N.i.R., 1960, No. 5; *V.P.P.S.*, 1958, No. 6;
Voprosi Filosofii, 1961, No. 3; 1964, No. 2;
House Without a Roof, by Maurice Hindus, 1961, p. 135;
Sovetskaya Estoniya, August 14th 1963

PART TWO

SHORT LIST OF AUTHORITIES

Baptist Times. September 27th, October 11th 1928; April 18th 1929

Blumit, Oswald *Sentenced to Siberia 1940*

Bolshakoff, Serge *Russian Nonconformity,* 1950

Byford, C. T. *Peasants and Prophets*
  The Soul of Russia, 1914

Eddy, Sherwood *Eighty Adventurous Years,* 1955

Hecker, J. F. *Religion under the Soviets,* 1927
  Religion and Communism, 1933

Hindus, Maurice *Broken Earth,* 1926
  Humanity Uprooted, 1929
  Red Bread, 1931
  House Without a Roof, 1961

Inkeles, A. *Soviet Society,* 1961

Kolarz, Walter *Religion in the Soviet Union,* 1961

Kügelgen, Carlo von (ed.) *The Whited Sepulchre,* 1935

Kolski, W. W. *The Soviet Régime,* 1954

Latimer, R. S. *Dr. Baedeker and His Apostolic Work In Russia,* 1907
  Under Three Tsars, 1909
  With Christ in Russia, 1910

Leroy-Beaulieu, A. *The Empire of the Tsars,* Vol. III, English ed.,
  1896

Noble, John and Everett, Glen *I Found God in Soviet Russia,* 1960

Prokhanov, I. S. *In the Cauldron of Russia,* 1933

Spinka, Matthew *The Church in Soviet Russia,* 1956

Stepniak *The Russian Peasantry,* English ed., 1905

Stretton, Hesba *The Highway of Sorrow in the 19th Century*
(Introduction by John Brown) *Stundists, The,* 1893

Timashev, N. S. *Religion in Soviet Russia, 1917–42,* 1943

Trotter, Mrs. E. *Lord Radstock*

PART THREE

REFERENCES WHERE NOT MENTIONED IN THE TEXT

Chapter XI

John Lawrence: *Frontier,* Autumn 1963
  Maurice Hindus: *House Without a Roof,* p. 133

Chapter XII

Maurice Hindus: *op. cit.*, p. 135
Red Star's complaint: April 5th 1959
Molodoi Kommunist's complaint: 1961, No. 2
Alexei Sibirko: *ibid.*
The drunkard's wife and the lonely new mother: *V.P.P.S.*, 1958, No. 6

Chapter XIII

The Tallinn debate: *N.i.R.*, 1961, No. 2
The Klapeida Conference: *Sovetskaya Litva*, November 23rd 1963
Discrimination at Dneprodzerzhinsk, etc.: *N.i.R.*, 1963, No. 4
The Preacher from Kolodnya: date is February 4th 1954
Medical Baptists: *N.i.R.*, 1962, Nos. 5, 6, 8

Chapter XIV

The anti-Baptist pamphlet was reviewed in *Sovetskaya Moldaviya*, November 27th 1963
Tikhomirov's story: *The Agitator*, November 19th 1962
Lada's story: *Red Star*

Chapter XV

References to christenings: *Partiinaya Zhizn*, 1963, No. 10; *Part: Zh: Kazakhstana*, May 1963; *Selskaya Zhizn*, June 5th 1963
The chemistry teacher at Tallin: date was December 26th 1963
Minister of Education: *N.i.R.*, 1963, No. 4
Komsomolskaya Pravda's comment on Sermons: September 1962
'It is incumbent on the school to fight . . .': *Sovetskaya Estoniya*, October 23rd 1963
Molodoi Kommunist wants parents in dock: date was October 1959
'A pickpocket takes . . .': *Red Star*, April 5th 1959
The headmaster from Chechen-Ingush A.S.R.: Moscow Home Service, July 19th 1962
Robert Malozemov: *Sovetskaya Rossiya*, June 9th 1963; *N.i.R.*, 1964, No. 2

Chapter XVII

'We Christians must co-operate . . .': *Bratsky Vestnik*, 1960, No. 2
Eleanor Lipper: *Eleven Years in Soviet Prison Camps*, 1951, pp. 144 ff.
'Pentecostalists' rolling on the floor: *Zarya Vostoka*, May 22nd 1961

Chapter XVIII

Voloshin: *Pravda,* September 1st 1962; *In the World of Nightmare,* 1962; *Izvestia,* June 20th 1962

Fedotov: *In the World of Nightmare,* Moscow Radio, April 10th 1963

Molokans in Transcaucasia: *Literaturnaya Gazeta,* October 30th 1958

Yakov and Olgo Stadel: *Komsomolskaya Pravda,* April 28th 1957

Trial of Ivan Zaporozhan: *Sovetskaya Moldaviya,* August 23rd 1963

Fyodor Myachin's book quoted Kolarz, *Religion in the Soviet Union,* pp. 334–5

Trial of N. P. Goretoi: *Pravda,* August 25th 1961

Chapter XIX

Atheist society denies elimination plans: see *N.i.R.,* 1963, Nos. 5 and 9. Also for details of closing of Orthodox churches

Baptist churches moved or temporarily closed in Siberia: *Bratsky Vestnik,* 1963, No. 2

The Postavy incident: *Sovetskaya Belorossiya,* October 19th 1963

Tula incident: *Izvestia,* January 23rd 1962

Chapter XX

Pochaev trial: *New York Times,* July 6th 1962

Istia trial: *Sovetskaya Kultura,* February 3rd 1962

Schuchinsk trial: *Kazakhstanskaya Pravda,* August 24th 1962

Kharkov trial: *Pravda Ukrainy,* June 19th 1962

Ashkabad trial: *Turkmenskaya Iskra,* September 8th 1962

Krivoy Rog, Zhdanov trials: Kiev Radio, September 28th 1962

Mary trial: *Turk: Iskra,* October 7th 1962

Ivanovka trial: *Sovetskaya Kirgiziya,* December 8th 1962

Semipalatinsk trial: *Kaz. Pravda,* December 12th 1962

Alma Ata trial: *Kaz. Pravda,* December 19th 1962

Smolensk trial: *Sovetskaya Rossiya,* December 22nd 1962

Belorussia trial: *Sov. Ross.,* December 17th 1962

Ussuri river trial: Vladivostok Radio, January 24th 1963

Tashkent trials: *Pravda Vostoka,* March 17th 1963, February 29th 1964

Brest trials: *Sov. Belorossiya,* May 13th 1963, March 11th 1964

Namangan trial: *Pravda Vostoka,* November 15th 1963

Yekabils trial: *Sov. Latviya,* March 5th 1964

Kulunda trial: *Sov. Yustitsiya,* May 1964